Praise for *A*

"Liz Kelly expounds on the powerful, final words Jesus spoke from the cross by effortlessly weaving together the autobiographical with stories about everyday people. In so doing, Kelly makes the historical event of the crucifixion more present and spiritually accessible to Catholics today. Reading it, one cannot help but experience more deeply the Father's love, which was definitively and unequivocally displayed at the crucifixion. A must read!"

—**Deacon Matthew Halbach, PhD, executive director of Catechesis, William H. Sadlier**

"We often focus on the triumph of the resurrection or the homely intimacy of the birth of Christ. Kelly directs our attention to the rawness of Golgotha and takes on the defining moment of human history, the death of Christ, with devotional care and theological insight. By meditating on Christ's words on the cross, Kelly opens our minds, touches our hearts, and inspires our knees to fall at the foot of the cross. Prepare to never read the crucifixion accounts in the same way."

—**Austin Suggs, host and creator of Gospel Simplicity, a YouTube channel where guests from across the Christian tradition bring simplicity out of theological complexity.**

"Liz Kelly has artfully woven together testimonies and reflections from Church writings to create a deeper journey into what Jesus said from the cross. How often have we heard these words read on Holy Thursday and Good Friday without taking the time to meditate on them? This book will engage the reader to deeper union with the transforming love of Jesus in his last moments. A great companion to take through the Lenten season."

—Julie Nelson, host of Catholic Women Now, Catholic women's speaker, www.julesforthecrown.com

"While the Bible has been a source of inspiration and comfort to me for years, there's something about the words of Jesus that touch me more than anything else. What a gift to have my Lord and Savior's words preserved in print! Out of all the recorded words of Jesus in the Bible, however, the words He spoke from the cross are especially meaningful to me. In *A Place Called Golgotha: Meditations on the Last Words of Christ*, Liz Kelly offers a fresh look at the final words of Jesus. Her reflections, prayer prompts, and discussion questions will lead you close enough to the foot of the cross that you'll hear Jesus speak directly to you!"

—Gary Zimak, bestselling author, speaker, radio host, FollowingTheTruth.com

"When reading *A Place Called Golgotha*, one is tempted to speed through to the end, because each page draws you into a progressively deepening encounter with Christ. But if you can proceed slowly and meditatively and allow yourself to savor the blessings of each chapter, your heart will be anointed. Liz Kelly's writing is pure gift to the work of expanding the kingdom."
—Jean Whelan, wife, mother, founder of the women's prayer and Scripture study group Mary's Women of Joy, and cohost of Joyful Echo on Carolina Catholic Radio.

"As we contemplate Jesus' last words, we become what we receive. In this wonderful book, Elizabeth Kelly invites each of us to receive the Father's regenerating Spirit who raised Jesus from the dead. As we speak Jesus' words *for us*, we are taken inside of them through contemplative prayer to discover that the Spirit is acting *through us*! We are drawn by Jesus' beauty to participate in making all things new (Rev. 21: 5)!"
—Fr. John Horn, SJ, author of *Heart Speaks to Heart: A Review of Life and Healing Prayer*

A Place Called
GOLGOTHA

Meditations on the
Last Words of Christ

ELIZABETH M. KELLY

Published by The Word Among Us Press

7115 Guilford Drive, Suite 100

Frederick, Maryland 21704

wau.org

26 25 24 23 22   1 2 3 4 5

ISBN: 978-1-59325-702-6

eISBN: 978-1-59325-703-3

Design by Suzanne Earl

Library of Congress Control Number: 2022920835

For my brother, Fr. Jon

"To die on the cross with Christ in order to be resurrected with him becomes a reality for every Christian and especially for every priest in the Holy Sacrifice of the Mass. Faith teaches that it is the renewal of the sacrifice on the cross. For those who, with living faith, offer or participate in the Mass, the same thing happens in and for them that happened on Golgotha."

—St. Teresa Benedicta of the Cross

Contents

CHAPTER 7

The Seventh and Final Word: *"Father, into your hands I commit my spirit."*

Introduction

As a child growing up in southern Minnesota farming country, I developed a great fondness for the spring melt.[1] The winter's snow ebbed slowly under the increasing heat of the spring sun as the days got longer, revealing that dark black, rich soil that had been buried beneath it for months. Spring in the country, long before the first seed is even planted, might bring one of the most delightful smells in the world. If "potential" had an aroma, that would be it.

My parents were not farmers, though we had a little land that a neighboring farmer cultivated for us, and we had fruit trees and a huge garden. Most of my friends were farm kids. They knew what it meant to toil in the heat of the sun or in the bitter cold of a Midwest winter; they knew what it meant to live under the reign of the unrelenting, unpredictable seasons. They worked hard on the land, and I admired this. Raised in the country surrounded by fields and groves, I developed a deep appreciation for growing things—and for those who knew how to make things grow.

Riding my horse through the spring fields, I would think about the seeds that would be planted deep within that dark soil, way down where no sunlight could reach them. Such a wonderful idea, that the life of this wheat or corn or bean would begin in utter darkness. What a supreme and delightful mystery, that somehow the seed knows to grow, to break through its shell and stretch upward, to slip its young savory limbs through all that blackness and greet the sun!

And this is a poignant reminder: new life often begins in total darkness. Somehow, in that wild convergence of nutrients and the raw materials of life, even though encased in a blackened tomb, the seed ruptures its skin and pushes up. The seed cannot feel the sun, cannot see it; still, all its energy is bent on the hope that once it breaches the topsoil, there the sun will be.

It is in this manner that we approach meditating with the last words of Christ on the cross: we enter into their darkness, trusting that there are spiritual nutrients to be extracted, nutrients that will help us grow through moments of darkness in our lives, graces and wisdom that will teach our souls to stretch upward, always in the direction of the Lord, to grow toward him rather than away from him, to find our flourishing in his light.

Our Interior Tragedy

"What were his last words?" We ask this sometimes, especially when someone of import dies, such as Pope St. John Paul II. We know that his last words were in Polish, his mother tongue. (How appropriate—he was already "going home.") Weakly he said, "Let me go to the house of my Father."

The pope's eyes were closed during one of the last Masses celebrated at his bedside, just days before he passed away. But at the moment of the consecration, he raised his right hand twice, marking the elevation of the Precious Body and Precious

Blood. We can look to our beloved pope in his death and learn so much about how to prepare for our own. I wonder, when it comes my time, will I be longing for my Father's house?

In some respects, this is the invitation of Lent; that is, we are invited to contemplate, to come to know Jesus, to keep him company in his passion, this most intimate personal space of all. And what a spectacularly generous gift. Because whom do you invite into your suffering but those you love the most? Whom do you call to your bedside, when you are sick and all hope is lost, but those you love and trust the most? Into this vulnerable sacred space, you invite your most trusted, most beloved friends.

What we discover when we contemplate Jesus' suffering is that he knows us in our suffering much more deeply than we know ourselves. Think about that: Jesus knows me in my suffering much more intimately than I know myself. He comes and kneels at the bedside of my suffering, and he pledges that he will not leave me. Though my suffering does not end, I am not alone in it. I will learn that it has the power to atone, to become redemptive—for me, for others, for the world.

In his reflection on the last words of Jesus, Fr. Robert Hugh Benson, the great English convert, asserts something very striking about our reverent consideration of the crucifixion. He says that "we are watching not just Christ's death but our own" death too, our own interior tragedy.[2] We might also assert that we are watching not just Christ's death, not just our death, but also our capacity to forgive: "Father, forgive them, not because they have apologized and made amends, but because they have no idea how seriously they have wounded me; they

"

What we discover when we contemplate Jesus' suffering is that he knows us in our suffering much more deeply than we know ourselves.

have no idea of the depth of damage they have wrought. Forgive them in their ignorance."

We also observe *our* capacity to surrender: "Into your hands I commit my spirit" (Luke 23:46, RSVCE); *our* deep longing for union with the Beloved: "I thirst" (John 19:28, RSVCE). We observe *our* right, our privilege perhaps, to call out to the Lord in times of mortal suffering: "My God, my God, why have you forsaken me?" (Matthew 27:46). We recognize our capacity to seek and receive the fullness of mercy: "Today you will be with me in Paradise" (Luke 23:43). We discover our capacity to serve to the very end, to love to the very end, and to see all things with eternal vision: "It is finished" (John 19:30).

Though this book is being released in time for the Lenten season, I hope it will find readership outside of Lent. I find that my own suffering does not have the courtesy to show up only during Lent; it is not liturgically minded. I hope the stories in these pages will offer support to anyone who wants to draw closer to Jesus during moments of spiritual darkness—that they may find nutrients and seeds of faith, hope, and love, always stretching toward the Son.

Gospel Accounts of the Death of Jesus

As I was working on this book, I often began the day by reading through the four Gospel accounts of the death of Jesus, one by one. I found it extremely fruitful to place them next to one another—it helped fill out the picture of this sacred event. As I did this, I could see more clearly the differences in the accounts of those last hours.

We sometimes wonder about these variations in the Gospel accounts, and that's worth discussing. The readings on the death of Jesus present an opportunity to address one of the more perplexing aspects of Scripture: that is, we know Scripture is true, but clearly each account emphasizes different aspects of the same event. Each author had special interests, audiences, and emphases; they wrote under the inspiration of the Holy Spirit for the Church universal and, at the same time, as individual writers with unique points of view. We bear in mind that, as Cistercian Fr. Roch Kereszty writes, the Gospels are not "modern biographies but testimonies. . . . [T]hey testify that God acted definitively in Jesus . . . and that Jesus himself is God."[3] Further, we know—the Gospel of John tells us explicitly (see John 21:25)—that many of the works and sayings of Jesus went unrecorded.

At any rate, the variations need not be unsettling, especially in light of what scholars tell us about the writing of the Gospels in those early days of the Church. I think about the fact that when a priest today gives his homily, three or four times over the weekend, it's not exactly the same every time, though his meaning is the same and we can trust that the Holy Spirit is at work in each homily. So, too, when Jesus spoke to the crowds, he probably didn't repeat himself verbatim, but we can trust that his meaning was transcendent, universal, eternal.

For example, we find four of the last words of Jesus in the Gospel of John, which probably indicates that John was close to these events. He stayed at the foot of the cross with Jesus until the end. On the other hand, Matthew's Gospel only records one word. It's all right that there are different expressions and emphases throughout the Gospels. This doesn't indicate contradiction but a multiplicity of viewpoints expressed through reliable inspired testimony.

I invite you to pause now, pick up your Bible, and prayerfully read the following passages in preparation for considering Jesus' last words on the cross. Ask God to speak to your heart as you rest with these scenes from the last hours of Jesus' life.

† **Matthew 27:32-55**
† **Mark 15:21-41**
† **Luke 23:32-49**
† **John 19:17-30**

CHAPTER 1

The First Word

"Father, forgive them, they know not what they do."
—Luke 23:34, NABRE

How significant it is that Christ begins his crucifixion calling upon heaven for forgiveness for those who would place him on that cross. Later we will consider the work of *receiving* forgiveness, but for this first word, we will focus on *offering* forgiveness.

Certainly the Father does not need coaxing or reminding to forgive the sins being committed against him and his Son. It's not a matter of Jesus trying to convince his Father of the right thing to do. We can assume that Jesus is simply claiming what is already taking place in heaven.

Furthermore, everything Jesus did and said wasn't for himself. He didn't need to actualize himself; rather, his words and works were for us. In this moment of radical forgiveness, we can see that he is aligning himself perfectly with the Father's will, with God's providence as it unfolds, and showing us that we must do the same.

The obvious question when considering the first word from the cross is this: Is the Lord really asking us to do as he does?

Does he expect us to forgive even the horrors of murder, betrayal, infidelity, the Holocaust—without conditions, without explanations, without receiving amends? You might think to yourself, "Jesus is God, and that's why he can forgive without any strings attached. I'm not God, and therefore he would never ask that of me."

Of course, Scripture is wildly demanding on this point—we cannot avoid, soften, or downplay it. Jesus' instruction on the subject is clear:

> Peter came and said to him, "Lord, if another member of the church sins against me, how often should I forgive? As many as seven times?" Jesus said to him, "Not seven times, but, I tell you, seventy-seven times." (Matthew 18:21-22)

It can seem like an impossible maneuver of heart to forgive in such a radical, freeing fashion. Here is how one woman did it, with the help of her Father.

A Choice to Live—and Help to Forgive[4]

They were expecting a big snowstorm that day. But in the early morning hours of March 3, 1985, brothers Tom and Joe, thirteen and fifteen respectively, began their Sunday as they always did: with a paper route.

"I had a big van," said the boys' mother, Joanne. "They used to love tossing the papers out of the back of that thing."

Later that morning, Joanne would head to a friend's house, with plans to meet her boys at a hockey banquet in the afternoon.

Her estranged husband, Robert, the boys' hockey coach, no longer lived at home but would come to her house and spend the day with their sons. Then they'd all meet up at the banquet.

Joanne, a dog handler, was just seventeen when she married, and the marriage had been difficult and abusive, eventually heading toward divorce. To avoid any turmoil during his visits, she would leave the house before he arrived. For all anyone knew, the Vietnam veteran was a good father who loved his children, took them hunting and fishing, and, according to his coworkers, was "a nice guy." Only the night before, he had joined the whole family at their home to celebrate Joe's fifteenth birthday.

As she drove away that morning, Joanne saw her husband's car approaching. He was early; she wondered why. That moment—passing his car on the freeway—haunts her to this day.

Sometime soon after, on that terrible snowy Sunday, Robert entered the home, shot and killed his two sons, three family dogs, and, later, in Joanne's bedroom, himself.

The Unthinkable Unfolds

As the snowstorm got stronger, Joanne called home to let her boys know she might be a few minutes late for the hockey banquet. She got no answer. She called a neighbor and asked him to deliver the message in person. He knocked and got no answer, so he entered the home.

A few steps in, he saw one of the dogs, lying dead. He immediately backed out, shut the door, and called the police. The next hours were like something out of a horror movie, as the police tried to determine if anyone was still in the house. After several hours, they shot in tear gas, entered, and discovered the extent of the tragedy.

A veritable army rose up to surround Joanne with help and support. Her father, along with her best friend, put on gas masks to enter the house and retrieve her insurance and other documents and try to salvage a few clothes. A friend with means paid for the funerals. Another, a businessman, walked Joanne through the insurance nightmare, which would stretch out for years.

Early in the investigation, Joanne was considered a suspect. "All my assets were frozen; I had nothing," she remembered, "[only] the clothes on my back." In her journal on March 9, 1985, she wrote:

> It's been almost a week. I still can't believe or understand. So many things to decide and do. So many people. So much evil yet so much love. I've asked God to pray for me now because I can't. I've asked him to give me the right answer I think he has. So much I don't understand or know yet. Little bits keep coming out. How they died, when, where, how long. I need to know all of it yet don't want to know.

At the time, Joanne would have referred to herself as a casual Catholic. She had a strong belief in God, it was important to her that her children receive a Catholic education, and she attended church, though not regularly. She didn't know it then, but the very tragedy that could easily have turned her away from God would instead turn her toward him, to radical forgiveness and a life of service.

A Walk along the River

In the months following the murders, Joanne lived with her parents. Returning to her home would be impossible for her emotionally, so she decided to build a new one. She bought a piece of land in a rural area in Wisconsin and rented a trailer to live in while the house was being built.

The location proved healing. Joanne had always felt God's presence in nature, and in that quiet countryside, she began to have many conversations with him in prayer. She also returned to regular Mass attendance, at a quiet country parish where the local priest befriended her and became a companion along the road back to living. "He'd say to me, 'You're Mary. You lost sons; she lost her son. Pray to Mary.'"

"It was good for me there," Joanne remembers, "because it was a little country church. People were very kind and quiet. . . . I became much more religious than I ever had been." She needed her faith to fight the self-pity, darkness, and depression that would threaten to cripple her in the days ahead.

A little over a year after the murders, Joanne took a walk along the river near her home. It was a moment that she would revisit many times in her mind and heart. "I had this clear sense of *You need to make a choice here. You need to choose to live.*"

She prayed for the strength to get up one more day, to somehow find a way forward. In the meantime, friends took up a collection to buy her a Labrador puppy, Skeet.

"I didn't think I would ever laugh again until Skeet came into my life," said Joanne. "But there she was, this little roly-poly fur ball."

Some solid counseling, Skeet, and lots of long walks along the river acted like a very gentle, steady, healing rain. After some years had passed, Joanne began working with Skeet and later other dogs, in pet therapy. She served in numerous hospitals and schools, quietly letting her dogs do the heavy lifting of reaching people who were trapped in trauma, illness, and grief. By far the most intuitive dog she worked with was a yellow Labrador, Trip.

"There was a doctor who hated the dogs in the hospital, but one day his nurse came running to find me," she recalled. He relayed the doctor's message: "I've got a patient, and he won't talk to any of us, he won't answer any questions, he won't tell us anything. One thing we do know is that he had a dog. Would you go in the room with him?"

Joanne and Trip went to work.

The patient was an elderly man, and initially he wouldn't acknowledge Joanne or the dog. So she pushed a big recliner next to the bed and put Trip in it. There's somebody here who really wants to see you," she announced to the patient. "You better roll over."

He did, and there sat the eighty-six-pound Trip.

"The nurses started whispering different questions to be asked," said Joanne, "and I would say, 'Trip wants to know this' or 'Trip wants to know that,' and he would talk to the dog. Everything they wanted to know, he told the dog."

For eight years Joanne toted Trip around the Minneapolis–St. Paul metro region, visiting the sick and the traumatized. "I've never seen an animal who knew so exactly what someone needed," she said.

God's Closet

Many describe grief as coming in waves, and in fact grief has visited Joanne in strong and unpredictable waves over the past thirty-eight years. There was a particularly challenging period, years after the death of her boys, during which she feared having a nervous breakdown. So in her imagination, she built a closet, and she filled it with the things she couldn't face. "It had a big black door and a gold doorknob," she recalled.

A psychologist encouraged Joanne to lock the door of the closet. "You never have to open it again. If you want to go in some time and take something out to look at it, you can."

Joanne speaks of her tragedy as "one of those pieces that you have to let go of." There's no way to reconcile it; there's no way to take that pain away. I believe that God gave me the ability to put it where I needed to put it, that he gave me the mind to create [that] closet, and . . . I don't need to worry about it; he's taking care of it. It's in his hands."

There were other things Joanne turned over to God, such as the extraordinary act of forgiveness.

"If the forgiveness piece was up to me, I don't know if I could do it," she said. "I had to let that be God's responsibility. I tell people it's not my job to forgive [Robert]; that's God's job. I have to let go of the anger. That's my job."

It would be hard to imagine a moment when "Forgive them, they know not what they do" could be more fitting. There would never be a moment of acknowledgment from her offender, never a moment she could confront him over what he had done, never a moment when he could apologize, explain himself, or ask forgiveness. And still forgiveness came. It is a gift Joanne says she received from the Lord.

"I really don't hate [Robert] anymore," she said. "I feel sadness, I feel pity, I often wonder what it was that could make someone do that. . . . But I don't harbor any anger toward him anymore."

Getting there was a long and painstaking process, full of lessons she is happy to share with others.

"I don't allow people to use the word [hate] in my house," said Joanne. "It's the worst four-letter word on the planet. It's like taking poison and expecting the other person to die. That's all you're doing [when you hate]; you're poisoning yourself."

Still, she has no illusions of perfectly complete healing this side of heaven.

"I don't think you ever feel like you make it through," she said. "It's like a wound. Today you have this gaping wound, and it's all you can think about. But pretty soon you see it starts to close, and you think about it, but it doesn't take your whole day. And pretty soon it's a scar, and you remember everything about it, but you don't think about it all the time. It's there, it's always there, it will always be a part of me, and I have to accept that."

Joanne, now seventy-three, eventually remarried and has two grown stepchildren and three step-grandchildren. She's survived three serious bouts of cancer. She starts each day with her Bible and Rosary. The Book of Job and Psalm 23 are favorites, as is the simple Hail Mary and Our Father. She prays constantly these days. And on her sons' birthdays every year, she asks Mary, the mother of Jesus, to give her boys a kiss.

"My two boys were so different," Joanne said, smiling. "My older boy was more like me, quiet and prone to stand back and watch things. My younger son was good-looking—all the girls loved him!—funny, outgoing, bubbly. . . . I often wonder what they would be like and what kind of kids they would have had."

These days, Joanne works with children eight to eighteen who want to train and show dogs. Smiling, she says, "These kids are wonderful. . . . I just love those kids. You see them change. They grow in confidence, they look you in the eye, they become self-confident."

When people who know her story ask her how she keeps going, Joanne will say, "How do you not? It's just this strong belief that there is a purpose and something I was put here to do or accomplish. "I want to remind people that evil can't take everything."

A Free Three-Legged Stool

More than a year goes by before I see Joanne again. As I step into her home, there is a new lightness in her, a new focus, and joy. Later I learn she has a new puppy—Mick, a beautiful English cocker spaniel with deep brown eyes. He looks older and wiser than a puppy, and she has hopes that he may one day develop into a fine service dog.

Even more significantly, Joanne's being asked to speak these days about her experiences. Her topic? "Hope," she says, smiling. Having worked in grief counseling earlier, she says, "Grief was my first genre, but now it's hope. And that's right; it should be about hope. The grief led me to it."

She tells me she's reading a great deal on the subject, especially her Bible. "'Hope' appears 167 times in the Bible," she says. "That really struck me."

To this day Joanne does not think in terms of having forgiven her husband herself. Rather, the Lord did that work for her and then offered it to her as a gift.

"He just did it," she says. "I don't even know how. It's a very slow process. You sense the lifting, a feeling of something being lifted from you. . . . That weight has been taken off of me slowly.

"People think that they are going to go to a support group or meet a therapist, or someone out there is going to wave a magic wand or give them the right words to make it all go away, and everything will be fine. But that won't happen. They have to choose. If they want to move forward, they have to choose."

And they have to actively work to receive and cultivate the virtues of faith, hope, and love, she says.

"It's like a three-legged stool. You can't have that stool with one of those legs missing. I work on it. I have faith, I have hope, and I have love, so I can construct that stool to sit on until I am reunited with my children. But if you are missing any part of that trio, you're on shaky ground."

Joanne has an accurate understanding of the infused virtues—faith, hope, and love—as free gifts given to us by the Holy Spirit. She says of hope in particular, "It's yours free. You can't buy it; it's a free gift. But you have to claim it. You can go

"

If you are struggling to forgive someone, give it time, and allow the Lord to do the heavy lifting for you, to offer forgiveness on your behalf until you can offer it on your own.

pick it up; it's waiting for you. You can bring it home. Wrap yourself in it like a blanket. Too many people leave their gift sitting on the shelf and never take it."

Her greatest hope is to see her boys again in heaven. "I'm not in a rush," she says, smiling, "but I do hope to see them again. I believe they are with God."

If you are struggling to forgive someone, struggling to forgive something even unforgivable, Joanne's story is an encouragement to give it time and to allow the Lord to do the heavy lifting for you, to offer forgiveness on your behalf until you can offer it on your own. In this way you can make the language of the Lord your own: "Father, please forgive them for me; they don't know what they've done. Forgive them for me, until I can forgive them in fullness and in freedom, too."

This first word from the cross is the key to unlock all the forgiveness you will ever need to offer. Turn to it as often as necessary. The grace in this word never runs out.

PROMPT FOR PRAYER

Forgive from the Heart:
An Imaginative Prayer Exercise

Our meditation will be anchored in Jesus' story of the forgiven slave who fails to forgive the debt of a fellow slave. Read Matthew 18:21-35. We must forgive, Jesus tells us, from the heart.

As I prayed with this verse, I asked Jesus to show me where I needed to forgive from my heart. I immediately thought of a relative who had never asked for forgiveness, never acknowledged his guilt, and now may never have the capacity to do so. Though I wanted to forgive him, I was having a hard time imagining how I could do that from my heart. What would that look like?

Then the Lord impressed upon me this image: I saw this man who had wounded me and my family, and he was standing with Jesus in front of a door. Behind the door was every sin the man had committed, even those he didn't know about or had never confessed. He now faced his life in complete and total honesty, without the chance to make excuses or offer explanations. The man looked frightened, like a little child about to be scolded. But the Lord stood there with him as he faced his life in truth; he would not leave the man an orphan.

There was something else behind this door: every ounce of forgiveness this man would need to get into heaven, forgiveness for everything left unconfessed or poorly confessed. In that moment, the Lord made it clear to me that I could help stockpile that room with forgiveness, with freedom. I could put into that room every ounce of forgiveness that I needed to offer, so that when this man opened the door and faced everything he had done, he would find the fullness of my forgiveness there, ready and waiting to wash over him like a fresh breeze on a putrid day.

I was filled with joy at this prospect of stockpiling forgiveness in advance. My heart was sincerely delighted at the thought that this man would find my forgiveness waiting there for him and would know that he was free. I started imagining filling the room with roses, blood red and fragrant. Then Jesus came to help me, multiplying every rose I placed by a hundred.

The roses grew in such volume that they peeked out of the cracks around the door, as though they were anxious to be discovered. There was so much beauty and joy and freedom—for me, for the Lord. We looked at each other, smiling at our fine work of filling the room with roses, and I felt like a little child opening a long-awaited gift.

I further wondered: is there someone, somewhere, stockpiling forgiveness for me? Will I find bitterness and resentment when I open the door, or will it burst open with blooms of forgiveness?

I encourage you to spend a few moments quietly reading Matthew 18:21-35. Pay attention to what captures your imagination: any word or phrase or idea. Rest in that.

Then gently ask yourself: is there someone I struggle to forgive?

Can you imagine this person standing with Jesus before the door that will reveal to them every wrong they have ever committed—and all the forgiveness they would ever need? Can you imagine stockpiling the forgiveness they would need from you? How does it feel to forgive them in advance of this moment?

Turn to Jesus. What is he doing? What does he say to you?

QUESTIONS FOR DISCUSSION OR JOURNALING

1. What struck you most about Joanne's story? What does her story stir in your heart?

2. Are you thinking about the gift of forgiveness in a new way? How?

3. Can you recall a moment when you struggled to forgive someone? What happened? If you were able to forgive, how did you get there? If you are still struggling to forgive, can you invite the Lord to do the work for you?

4. What happens when you imagine Jesus forgiving on your behalf?

CHAPTER 2

The Second Word

"Truly I tell you, today you will be with me in Paradise."
—Luke 23:43

When I lived in Alaska, I wrote for the Sunday magazine section of the local paper. My feature, "We Alaskans," highlighted Alaskans with unusual occupations. One woman, an artisan, made wooden dolls by hand. Another gentleman crafted cedar-strip wooden canoes, one-of-a-kind works of incredible beauty that attracted buyers from around the world. Another was a professional clogger.

One interview that always stood out for me was with a prison guard at a maximum-security prison for men. I'll never forget the day I visited that prison. It was a beautiful, bright spring day. Break-up of all the ice and snow was officially underway, and we were gaining minutes more sunlight every day. Spring in Alaska is a wondrous and hopeful thing, like a spectacular, brilliant earth eruption. I was aware of all this as I drove through the woods to meet with the guard.

Pulling into the facility, I was struck by how drab and lifeless it was. The immovable concrete building stood in stark contrast to the life and loveliness of its surroundings. Entering the prison—passing one set of guards, then another, moving through gate after gate, each slamming behind me with a heavy and hard cruelty—my heart sank with the bitter reality its occupants faced, some for life.

Finally the guard took me into the section that housed inmates who had committed the most violent crimes. These lived in isolation twenty-three hours of the day, with only an hour for exercise and recreation outside their cells. They were all present in their cells as I entered but behind plexiglass windows—not bars, as I'd expected from the prison movies I'd seen. There were several tiers of cells overlooking a large room with tables and chairs. It reminded me of stepping into a mall to go window shopping, except the windows were occupied by men, not merchandise.

When I came into view, many of the prisoners rushed up to their windows, put their hands on the glass, and stared at me wide-eyed. It startled me, and the guard said, "Yeah, they haven't seen a woman in a long time."

I remember thinking to myself, these are not men. Maybe they once were, but they weren't anymore. They were more like animals, caged and tense in the complete absence of human touch. "How does one end up like *this*, in *this* terrible place?" I wondered.

I can't imagine any of those men as little boys, dreaming of one day becoming a criminal. They must have had dreams like those of other boys—of becoming pilots or mountaineers, firemen or fishermen. I don't imagine that many of them turned from innocent children into hardened and violent criminals in an instant. It was probably years of abuse or neglect that told them they were worth nothing and what they did was of no consequence to the world.

I imagine that many of these men have a long line of people they need to forgive: maybe parents and family, those entrusted with their care who were, for whatever reason, unable to teach a little boy that he was unique and unrepeatable, that God had a plan for his life, that there was a way forward by which he would flourish in the art of being human and know the tender joy of being loved by God. I imagine that in most cases, there was more than one person to blame, perhaps a whole community of people who contributed to the eventual incarceration of these men.

Still, each of them had committed some terrible crime. At some point they exercised their free will—to the degree that it was in fact free—and took another life, perhaps in a subconscious and secret revenge for the life they never got to have. I do not excuse their crimes; I do not wish to lessen the consequences of the choices they made and how dreadfully that affected other lives and families. But I do marvel that we are all made of the same stuff, with the potential to become a Mother Teresa or a murderer.

How tenuous life is, how important the decisions of those entrusted with our formation when we are young and vulnerable. How important our own decisions are, setting us on a trajectory toward heaven or hell, even hell on earth. And this makes me wonder about "the good thief."

The Mercy of Today

The Gospel of Luke records the moment of encounter between Christ and the thieves crucified beside him:

> One of the criminals who were hanged there kept deriding him and saying, "Are you not the Messiah? Save yourself and us!" But the other rebuked him, saying, "Do you not fear God, since you are under the same sentence of condemnation? And we indeed have been condemned justly, for we are getting what we deserve for our deeds, but this man has done nothing wrong." Then he said, "Jesus, remember me when you come into your kingdom." He replied, "Truly I tell you, today you will be with me in Paradise." (23:39-43)

It is impossible to miss the extraordinary mercy that Jesus unleashes in this word: the unimaginable forgiveness and, what's more, the astonishing invitation to intimate friendship with Jesus in eternal joy. We cannot for certain know the sins of the robber, though scholars indicate he was probably an insurrectionist, violently resisting Roman authority.[5] Perhaps this was a point of connection for the good thief: both he and Jesus were an affront to Roman rule, though Jesus never used violence.

The sins of the thief are no obstacle to the forgiveness and mercy of Jesus, nor to friendship with him. His reply to the thief who begs to be remembered is not "Today you will be in purgatory," nor "Someday soon, when you have been purified, then you can join me in heaven." No: *today, paradise.* The thief's conversion must have been a thing to behold.

Jesus' words are especially moving when we consider that earlier in the day, the Gospel of Matthew tells us, the two thieves together mocked and reviled the Lord (see 27:44). What kind of an encounter must the good thief have had with Jesus in those few hours that would cause such a compelling and total conversion, a change of heart so pure that Jesus would offer him not just forgiveness but eternity in his glorious company? What did the good thief witness that swung him in the other direction so quickly and completely?

We can guess that, at the very least, he heard Jesus cry out to the Father, begging forgiveness for those who crucified him. As the good thief witnessed this supreme act of forgiveness, did it create a fissure in his heart, just the tiniest crack of wonder and awe? Was that all he needed for Truth to find its way in and all of heaven to flood his heart with recognition?

This man suddenly understood whose presence he was in, the one true God made visible and accessible through Jesus Christ. This priceless recognition came with the hope that maybe there was forgiveness for him, too.

Pope Benedict XVI wrote of eternal life as a "relational event." He explained, "Man did not acquire it from himself or for himself alone. *Through relationship with the one who is himself life, man too comes alive.*"[6]

This is precisely what we witness in the good thief. Perhaps for the first time and in the most dire and cruel of circumstances, he *recognized* "the one who is himself life." At that moment, the good thief truly came alive.

Another Good Thief

Conversion is personal; it comes about in various ways. St. Paul fell to the ground as he heard Jesus call to him (see Acts 9:1-18). St. Augustine was sitting in a garden when he heard a child nearby chanting, "Take up and read." Taking up the Letters of St. Paul that were nearby, Augustine read Paul's admonition to "make no provision for the flesh, to gratify its desires" (Romans 13:14), and his conversion was complete.[7] St. Josephine Bakhita had faith in God from her earliest days, but she endured abduction from her family and years as a slave before she met Jesus through a spiritual benefactor. Ève Lavallière, the acclaimed French actress of the early 1900s, left a life of wealth and fame to live as a joyful penitent through the friendship of a country priest who taught her the faith.

We can never have enough examples of that breakthrough moment: *recognition*. In more recent days, we have been blessed with the publication of the prison letters and journals of the young Frenchman Jacques Fesch. These reveal a soul earnestly searching for the truth. *Light over the Scaffold: Prison Letters of Jacques Fesch* and *Cell 18: Unedited Letters of Jacques Fesch* (St. Paul Publications, 1996) provide an intimate view not only of a "good thief" conversion but also of the unfolding of the life of an unlikely mystic.

On April 6, 1930, Jacques was born into a loveless and sometimes violent household. Jacques's father was a bank president with a cold, tyrannical personality. Jacques's biographer wrote that his father "made family life unbearable. He paid little or no attention to his son, save for a systematic attempt to destroy in the child all his enthusiasm, confidence, optimism, and faith."[8] Jacques's mother was no refuge, as she had little capacity for the kind of intimacy and support that motherhood demanded.

Jacques's father and mother often engaged in screaming matches, and his father frequently abused alcohol. Though Jacques spent a few years in Catholic school as a child, his father was a staunch atheist; Jacques described him as having "a disgust for life."[9] Jacques grew up in an environment that offered little hope and virtually no moral grounding. He was left to his own inadequate devices to create a way forward for himself.

During military service, Jacques met Pierrette, and when she became pregnant, they married. As he later commented, neither he nor his wife were mature enough for marriage, much less parenthood. Jacques followed military service with some overtly deceitful schemes and several botched attempts at work. Failing at work and family life, he eventually left his wife and daughter and floundered still further, dreaming of escape. A friend suggested he buy a boat and flee to the high seas, where adventure and the freedom he so desperately craved awaited him.

It was at this point, lost and hopeless, that a poisonous idea began to brew in Jacques's mind. He reflected on this moment from prison:

Everything conspired to make me flee, to take the broad road leading to perdition. With each passing day the net tightened around me, the net which was to stifle me in the end. A hunted soul! My wife was a living reproach to me because I had abandoned her. My mother, seeing the sorry success of my work, had driven me from her home. Then there were the business associates to whom I had to render accounts . . . [and who] told me, "Sell the car, pay your debts, return to your wife, swallow your pride, and go out and look for a job." But where would I get the strength to make such a costly decision? Would I get it from the cynicism, the nihilism that had inculcated me? . . . I was convinced that ultimate chaos was sure to defeat all my schemes. . . . No, flight was preferable.[10]

To sail away from everything and everyone; to leave behind every failure, every disappointment, every painful memory. The idea, disguised as a tonic, took hold of Jacques, like an aggressive cancer bent on devouring its victim.

The Crime

In February 1954, Jacques decided he would rob a money changer in order to acquire his boat to freedom. He later admitted that he turned to the idea of stealing the money with little hesitation. But the robbery he planned, and planned poorly at that, devolved into a crime far more tragic.

Jacques took a gun from his father's house and later armed himself with a hammer as well. On the day of the incident, he stood outside the money changer's shop, pacing back and forth, arguing with himself, calling off the crime and then returning to it. Finally, convinced this was the only way forward, he and an accomplice entered the money changer's place of business.

Jacques struck the businessman on the head with the butt of his revolver. The man, stunned and bleeding, managed to call out.

The gun went off accidentally, wounding Jacques's hand. Now he was bleeding. He grabbed what money he could—a few bills—the money changer yelled for help, and a chase ensued. Separated from his accomplice, Jacques hid for a short time, but someone spotted him, so he ran.

A policeman called for Jacques to stop and raise his hands. He didn't. Panicked, bleeding, and in utter confusion, Jacques, who had poor eyesight and was no marksman, turned and fired one shot, which went straight through the policeman's heart, killing him. Jacques ran on, and he shot another man, seriously wounding him.

The police caught up with Jacques at a subway station. He recalled later the sickening refrain running through his mind in that moment: "What have I done? What have I done?"

A Personal Conversion Trinity

It can be easy to shrug off a prison conversion as something manufactured to coerce others to pity, but there is nothing insincere in Jacques's letters and journal entries. In fact, they bring readers to deeper conversion. At no point does Jacques shrink from the horrors of his crime, though he unravels how he arrived at it. It was not one poorly chosen step but a lifetime of circumstances that led the troubled young man to pull the trigger. His authentic examination of conscience led him to deep remorse and all the suffering that accompanies sincere repentance.

Reading Jacques's story can help us appreciate the conversion of the good thief at Golgotha. What took place for the good thief in three hours took place for Jacques over three years. His is a testimony to the healing power of friendship and the importance of embracing moments of divine recognition. The circumstances of Jacques's early life helped land him in a prison cell; but through the circumstances of that cell, God the Father reclaimed him, remade him, and brought him home.

In prison Jacques was confined in isolation. His half-hour walk each day was also in solitude. He could write letters, up to sixty lines a day, and he had half an hour each week in the parlor. He was permitted one package a month, three books a week, and an unlimited number of letters. His daily routine was bleak, especially in the beginning.

But living in isolation, with hours each day to read and reflect, Jacques seemed to be less in a prison cell and more in a cloister. His circumstances were state-imposed and far from desirable, no doubt, but a he lives in a kind of cloister for self-examination and discovery nonetheless.

When the prison chaplain visited him initially, Jacques sent him away, indicating that he had no faith in anything. Remnants of his father's stern atheism still guided the young criminal. The chaplain didn't give up but continued to visit. Intent on engaging Jacques in dialogue and friendship, he eventually began to lend him books on the faith. This priest was the first person of what became Jacques's personal conversion trinity.

The second person was Brother Thomas, a childhood friend of Jacques's wife, Pierrette. Thomas belonged to a religious order, and he lived with great joy the austere rhythms of a monk's life. He was also one of Jacques's primary correspondents, doing what he could to share his religious life and prayer with the young prisoner. Jacques often commented that he prayed the hours with Brother Thomas or, after Thomas was ordained, joined in prayer as Fr. Thomas celebrated Mass. Jacques wrote to his mother-in-law that Fr. Thomas "knew how to read between the lines and immediately understands the state of a soul."[11] The two men developed a deep brotherly affection and a kind of spiritual symmetry over the years of their correspondence.

Jacques's lawyer, Paul Baudet, was the third person of Jacques's rescue crew. A Christian who served his clients with zeal, Baudet personally involved himself in Jacques's conversion. Jacques frequently comments in his letters on the encouragement and faithfulness of his lawyer. During the trial, in particular, Jacques recognized Baudet's refusal to engage in any kind of exaggeration or drama. These were tactics the prosecution readily took up, describing Jacques as a ferocious mastermind intent on murder from the start. Baudet fought hard for his client with utmost integrity, and Jacques took note.

Together these three men formed a community in which Jacques could experience, perhaps for the first time in his life, true Christian friendship and what it means to be a Christian man.

Remarkably, Pierrette never abandoned Jacques. She visited him faithfully, brought pictures of their daughter, Veronica, and never gave up on the idea that Jacques's life might be spared. Throughout his years in prison, Jacques was reintroduced to his daughter and expressed fatherly affection in letters and drawings for her. His mother-in-law, whom he addressed as "Mama" in his letters, was also a faithful correspondent. She and Jacques wrote to one another almost daily, and Jacques made it clear that her letters were "the center of every day for me, and without them I should have suffered deeply."[12]

Uncommon Faith

During that first year in prison, Jacques examined himself and his life. And though he didn't even know it and wouldn't have expressed it this way, he began to put on a new armament, replacing his revolver with the mustard seed of faith and shedding hopelessness for a burgeoning trust in his new friends. He read Scripture, which he came to love and quote easily, frequently, and at length in his letters. "Little by little," he wrote, "I was led to change my ideas. I was no longer certain that God did not exist. I began to be open to Him, though I did not as yet have faith. I tried to believe with my reason, without praying, or praying ever so little."[13]

Jacques received a book about Mary, the mother of Jesus, that moved him deeply. In letters as yet unpublished, he describes an encounter with her that led him to an ardent Marian devotion by which he was spiritually re-mothered.

As he approached the marking of his first full year in prison, Jacques crept closer and closer to conversion and repentance. Soon enough he was ready for absolution and reception of the Blessed Sacrament. He wrote of this time:

> At the end of my first year in prison, a powerful wave of emotion swept over me, causing deep and brutal suffering. Within

the space of a few hours, I came into possession of faith, with absolute certainty. I believed and could no longer understand how I had ever not believed. Grace had come to me. A great joy flooded my soul, and above all a deep peace. In a few instants everything had become clear. It was a very strong, sensible joy.[14]

In a letter to Brother Thomas not long after this experience, he further described his conversion:

An immense grief and an immense joy sweep over the soul together, and for the first time I have wept tears of joy, knowing with certitude that God has forgiven me and that now Christ lives in me through my suffering and my love. . . . I admit that I am still a very tepid Christian, repentant certainly and full of good will, but without much will power. I so need His love, strength, and compassion. . . . I beg Him to live in me always, to help and enlighten me and to give me the strength to accept the sufferings His mercy has willed to send me for the sake of my birth into the light, to me, who helped to sink the nails into His hands. But with Him there is mercy, and because of His law I have hoped in Him.[15]

Jacques had been introduced to the narrow way that leads to life, and even the looming threat of death by guillotine would not turn him from it.

His days took on a disciplined rhythm of reading, reflection, prayer, and writing, as Jacques grew steadily toward a mature faith life. His remaining two years in prison were awash in the waves of faith that most believers experience: days of ardor and joy, days of purification and suffering, days of aridity, days of peace. But Jacques's faith, born of tragic circumstances, was not a common one. His last days reflect not only the conversion of a good thief, not only a father and husband now concerned with the souls of his wife and child, not only a son offering his life for the conversion of his father, but the inner struggle and triumph of a mystic.

Into the Upbuilding Furnace

Jacques was facing the death penalty, and as the trial drew near, it seemed clear that his conviction would be used to set an example for other criminals. Further, he had killed a police officer, and the police union was exacting some influence on his penalty. As the trial commenced, the prosecution relentlessly pounded the jury with the word "killer, killer, killer." The jury rendered a guilty verdict, and the court denied Jacques's appeals. He would be executed by guillotine within a few months.

Jacques's writings from his last days reveal that God was inviting him into some of the deepest experiences of the spiritual life. Among these were the mysteries of forgiveness—both giving and receiving it—and the work of redemptive suffering. These mysteries settled on Jacques—teaching him, forming him, purifying him, furthering his conversion. He found the purification process excruciating at times:

> I am being tried like gold in the furnace. . . . [F]irst, powerful thrusts toward the light are followed by passing darkness; second, there are more or less lengthy phases of abandonment in which all joy disappears and only aridity is left. At the moment

I am being left to myself, although supported by His strength, and I am waiting patiently for the Lord to draw me to Himself once more, and to place me on a summit a little higher than the last one.

From day to day I ascend toward God, or rather, allowing His grace to act in me, I am being lifted up to that destined place from which I shall fly to paradise. I pray without ceasing, but of course during these periods of abandonment my prayer is less continual and many spontaneous acts of union are wanting to my days, so much so that I feel I am slipping a little. I assure you that I am aware of the degree of purification needed before one can be admitted to contemplation of the Lord!

Jesus is adorning my soul. He banishes the slightest evil thought and sharpens my sensitivity and enlightens my conscience so that I can work with Him in this upbuilding. I have been in the depths of agony for nearly two months and realize clearly how impossible it is for souls to win paradise without total submission. Jesus does everything, and I let Him do it, even if it causes me some pain. I am waiting until all shall be ready for the fruit He Himself has planted to be gathered, and I lose myself in the contemplation of His infinite love.[16]

Jacques began to accept his sentence with courage and an earnest desire to offer his life in atonement for his sins. He recorded on more than one occasion that the Lord had promised him all the graces he would need on the day of his execution. Truly, in Jacques's agony, Jesus never fell asleep. He stayed awake with him and kept him close company, helping him place his imminent demise in the context of eternity.

Jacques wrote to Brother Thomas:

It is not I who am advancing toward Him, but He who once more carries me on His shoulders. . . . [I]t is not death I am approaching, but life. . . . Strength is being poured into my soul in good measure, pressed down and running over. Who can describe the marvels of the Lord? I have two months ahead of me, and I know now what Jesus wants of me: total surrender of my will to His, and the positive acceptance of this penalty which had once aroused my rebellion. Just or unjust, it no longer matters. Everything is forgiven, all is superabundantly redeemed, all is confidence, now, in the infinite power of His mercy.[17]

Jacques spent his last two months praying, writing many letters, receiving Communion when he could, and seeing those visitors who were allowed. He fervently believed that at the time of his death, "I will be carried straight to paradise with all the gentleness lavished on a newborn babe."[18]

The Final Hours

Jacques spent most of the night before his execution in prayer, visited by moments of terror and doubt. As he prayed, his fear gave way to moments of surrender, peace, and confidence in the Lord's forgiveness and mercy. He wrote,

At the last, in the light of faith, I accept the cross, which gradually becomes so light I scarcely feel it. I offer up my suffering, the injustices done to me. I love those who strike me, and I know that one day I shall hear these words, like the good thief on the cross, "Amen I say to you, this day you will be with Me in paradise."[19]

His final journal entry was perhaps most moving of all:

In five hours, I shall see Jesus! How good He is, our Lord! He doesn't even wait until eternity to reward His chosen ones. He draws me ever so gently to Himself, giving me a peace which is not of this world.[20]

Jacques awoke at 3 a.m. on the day of his execution, said his prayers, and made his bed. He refused the final glass of rum and cigarette traditionally offered to those about to be executed and instead received final absolution and the Blessed Sacrament. The priest who attended him later wrote that as Jacques approached the scaffold, he remembered the crucifix the priest had with him and said, "Father, the crucifix!" These were his last words. The priest presented the crucifix to Jacques, who kissed it many times.

Jacques Fesch was guillotined at 5:30 in the morning, October 1, 1957. He was twenty-seven years old.

Facing Up to Who We Are

In some measure, we are all the good thief. We need constant conversion, realignment with our Creator, and the courage to face the damage that our sins have wrought. We need to hang there in agony with Jesus in his suffering, in ours, looking fearlessly at what our sin does in the world.

"

Jesus can find us
no matter where we are,
no matter what barriers
we think keep him from us.
He found Jacques Fesch in
prison; he found the good
thief on the cross.

And we are the good thief who can beg for the Lord's forgiveness—even for those sins we hate to admit. We can trust that God's forgiveness is rushing toward us at every moment, as it did toward the good thief, even before our recognition of him is purified, even before our surrender is whole, even while our repentance is unworthy. God is rushing toward us even now with forgiveness—even now with a taste of paradise, *today*.

Jesus can find us no matter where we are, no matter what barriers we think keep him from us. He found Jacques Fesch in prison; he found the good thief on the cross. He can find you, however dark it might be where you are. There is no place he would not go, no pain he would not endure, in order to find you, to rescue you, to claim you, and to bring you home. Indeed, he has endured all already—just for you.

PROMPT FOR PRAYER

Praying for the Graces Given to the Good Thief

Prayer Exercise One

The good thief received the grace that allowed him to recognize Jesus. Pray for that grace of recognition, that you might come to know Jesus better and to understand who he is.

Then spend a few moments meditating on John 21:1-9, in which the Lord appears to the disciples after his resurrection. They are out fishing when he tells them to lower their nets on the right side of the boat. As they haul in a big catch, Peter recognizes Jesus, exclaiming, "It is the Lord!" (21:7).

As you pray with this passage, place yourself in the scene. Fr. Timothy Gallagher would tell us to see the persons, hear the words, and observe the action.[21] What does this passage stir in you? Have there been times when you clearly recognized the presence of the Lord in your life? What happened, and how did it affect you?

Prayer Exercise Two

Ask for the grace of a deeper sense of God's mercy as you pray with this passage from Ezekiel:

> Thus says the Lord GOD: I will gather you from the peoples, and assemble you out of the countries where you have been scattered, and I will give you the land of Israel. When they come there, they will remove from it all its detestable things and all its abominations. I will give them one heart, and put a new spirit within them; I will remove the heart of stone from their flesh and give them a heart of flesh, so that they may follow my statutes and keep my ordinances and obey them. Then they shall be my people, and I will be their God. (11:17-20)

Do you need the mercy of Jesus in a particular area of your life? Is there a place in your heart that feels stony and unchangeable? Or is there a situation in which you need to offer mercy to another? Speak to the Lord about these things.

† † †

QUESTIONS FOR DISCUSSION OR JOURNALING

1. What struck you most about Jacques's story? Did you find his conversion credible, compelling? Why or why not?

2. Can you recall a moment of conversion in your life? What happened? How did you change as a result?

3. Recall a moment when you had a clear sense of receiving the Lord's forgiveness and mercy. What happened? How do you know you were forgiven?

CHAPTER 3

The Third Word

"Woman, here is your son." . . . *"Here is your mother."*
—*John 19:26, 27*

A few years ago, I took my mother on retreat. The priest who directed the retreat told the following story during one of his homilies.

He had been a priest for some years when the father of a family friend passed away, and the family requested that he return home to celebrate the funeral Mass. He didn't want to honor that request for one important reason. He knew that the priest currently assigned to the parish was young and new, still settling into the life of the priesthood and into his parish. That priest was from another country, and he was still under the terrible strain of learning a second language. It wasn't easy for his parishioners to understand him, and this created an added barrier to his settling into the parish.

The older priest knew that funerals were a prime opportunity for getting to know your parishioners in a more intimate way than was possible through regular Sunday Masses. He didn't want to rob the younger priest of this experience of tending to his flock when they were grieving. So as difficult as it was, he declined the family's request.

Undaunted by this reply, the family took a different tack. They turned instead to the older priest's mother. A few days later, he received a call from his mother, who simply said, "Son, I wouldn't dream of telling you what to do, but it would sure be nice if you could come and celebrate the funeral mass."

You could almost hear the echoes of the wedding feast at Cana, the gentle voice of Jesus' mother, saying, "Son, I wouldn't dream of telling you what to do, but it would sure be nice if they didn't run out of wine."

As you might guess, the older priest returned home. Placing the younger priest at the center of his flock as often as possible, he concelebrated the funeral Mass and offered the funeral homily—because his mother asked him to.

No one knows you the way your mother does. And no one seems to have the same kind of affect and influence on you. Maybe that is because of the singularity of your mother's experience: she had you all to herself for nine very important months while you were being formed into the fullness of a human being: growing heart and lungs, flesh and bone, hands and feet—feet that occasionally kicked her, no less. She literally kept you alive throughout this vulnerable process with her own blood. Your blood was first her blood.

When Jesus says, "Woman, here is your son," we might wonder just what he's up to. Is he severing a tie? Why would he do that to one who was so essential to his life?

Rather, I think this word offers us an invitation to know Mary, Virgin Mother, in new ways—to know her much more closely, more as Jesus did, with all the intimacy that implies. This word isn't the severing of a relationship but the reordering and expansion of one. This moment at the foot of the cross, when Jesus seems to give Mary away, to entrust her to John and John to her, is an exceptionally powerful moment for asking ourselves if our suffering is refining, possibly expanding, our own role in our families, communities, the Church, and the world.

"And the Word Became Flesh *Here*"

Soon after I finished the Spiritual Exercises of St. Ignatius of Loyola, I had the opportunity to go to the Holy Land with a small group. God was exceptionally generous: the Exercises turned out to be wonderful preparation for that pilgrimage because when you enter into the Exercises, you enter deeply and prayerfully into the gospel.

So when I got to the Holy Land, I felt that, in some ways, I'd been there before—in my imagination and in my prayer. Still, I would return home with a heightened sense of how little I had drawn upon the fullness of Scripture, how little I knew of the Church's Jewish heritage, and how important it is to claim that connection.

Most unexpectedly, I also gained a new awareness of who Mary is. As I was preparing for the trip, I had a sense that I should make this pilgrimage, not just for myself, but for my mother, who would never get to visit the Holy Land, and for all the women in my life. I carried their intentions with me everywhere I went. And it was almost as if heaven reached down to help me carry them.

One friend gave me an intention to place in the Wailing Wall. The day we were there, she later informed me, happened to be her birthday. We celebrated Mass on Calvary, within the Church of the Holy Sepulchre, on Mother's Day—hardly a coincidence to my mind. That same day we visited Dormition Abbey, built over what is believed to be the apostle John's home. Mary would have spent her last days there before being assumed into heaven. Given that I was praying for my mom and my women friends, these moments resonated in my heart.

Even more, the incredible living sites of the Holy Land—the waves of the Sea of Galilee, the lovely ancient olive trees in the Garden of Gethsemane, the starkness of the desert and the Mount of Temptation—were no longer an abstraction, something I had to imagine. I could walk where Jesus walked and pray where Jesus prayed. And I started to understand that the greatest gift that Mary gives us is this: because of Mary, Jesus is no longer an abstraction. He is real, he is flesh and blood, we can touch him, and he can touch us in a real way because of Mary's generosity. The very blood of Jesus was first his mother's. The very blood of Jesus—this blood he would shed on the cross for our sins—was first Mary's blood.

In *Jesus of Israel: Finding Christ in the Old Testament*, Fr. Richard Veras relates this very useful story:

A good friend of mine was visiting her daughter and grand-daughter one weekend. There was an awkwardness when Sunday morning came, because my friend is Catholic, and her daughter left the Church for an Evangelical church that is suspicious of Catholic teaching. As my friend was leaving for Mass, her four-year-old granddaughter begged to go with her. The young girl's mother begrudgingly allowed it.

After Mass, as grandmother and granddaughter were leaving the church, the girl noticed a statue in the middle of the lawn.

"What's that, Grandma?"

"It's a statue of Mary."

"Who's Mary?"

The shocked grandma responded, "The mother of Jesus!"

The equally shocked granddaughter replied, "Jesus had a mother?"

In that moment, for that little girl, Jesus became human. Someone whom she had learned about as Lord had become like her in all things but sin. She could relate to him now as she never could before.[22]

Mary, this anonymous Jewish girl—formed in her faith to anticipate the Messiah—assented to the work of the Holy Spirit within her, and so we no longer have to imagine him. Because of Mary's yes, Jesus is no longer an abstraction. He is real and truly available to us as friend, teacher, healer, and Lord.

In a rare moment of grace, I had the opportunity to pray in the church built over the site where the angel Gabriel appeared to Mary. This spot is usually mobbed with visitors, but I found myself there with the woman leading the pilgrimage, just the two of us, for about twenty minutes. On our knees, we prayed, "Be it done unto me!" It was awesome.

Carved on the marble altar in that church are the familiar Latin words *Verbum caro factum est*, "And the Word became flesh." Only here the phrase is *Verbum caro hic factum est,* "And the Word became flesh here"—right here, in this place (or at the very least, somewhere nearby). And kneeling there, praying for all the women I carried in my heart, praying to Mary, through Mary, I could very nearly feel the flutter of Gabriel's wings.

Fr. Gerald Vann, OP, writes in his exquisite meditation *The Divine Pity*:

> You have in Mary, the Mother of mercy, the figure of what you have to be. It may be particular men—husband, children, friends—who will come to you so; it may be your vocation to share with Mary something of her universal pity, but to renew the soil of the world only indirectly, through your own inner experience and unexpressed pity. But somehow, in some way, you must share her vocation, you must share the glory of the destiny of which she is the symbol and the supreme expression; for only so can you share as you should in the restoring of the world, and only so will you yourself be made whole.[23]

You see, this is what Mary does: she brings Jesus to us. Salvation has a mother, and more than anything, this mother wants to introduce you to her child. She wants you to come to know her son, Jesus, just as intimately as she does, in a flesh-and-blood way.

So how is that going? Are you in a season of coming to know Jesus better, in a more personal way? Is Mary helping you in this relationship?

Full Blossom, Full Bloom

On the last day of an Ignatian retreat that I attended, the retreat director invited us to pray with the Scriptures that focus on Christ's resurrection. In his writings, St. Ignatius of Loyola proposes that Christ appeared first to his mother after his resurrection. Even though the Gospels don't record such an encounter, Ignatius suggests it's logical to assume it took place—given Mary's holiness, her role in the young Church, and her relationship with her son. Ignatius asks us to prayerfully meditate on what this moment might have been like.[24]

And so I meditated on the Easter morning shared between Mary and Jesus. As I did, the encounter played out before me, almost like a movie on a screen. Immediately the scene went into rewind, starting not with Easter morning but with Good Friday night.

The women have brought Mary to her room, where there's a basin with water and a cloth with which she can wash herself. She's covered in her son's blood; it stains her clothes and her skin. Looking down at the basin, she can barely bring herself to consider washing away the precious blood of her son. The idea of giving up this last remnant of him fills her with impenetrable sorrow.

Eventually, Mary begins to wash, slowly and carefully, and as she does, the blood turns the water red. Then she removes her outer clothes; she cannot bring herself to wash them. She has to think about what she'll do with them, maybe bury them. But for now, she folds them and puts them on her bed.

Putting on a white robe over her night clothes, she returns to the basin. She's thinking about what to do with the water, now commingled with her son's blood. She decides to pour out this blood and water in the garden, on the roots of a young tree she can see from her bedroom window. She takes the basin to the garden, empties it, and watches as the ground absorbs the contents. For a moment, she wants to disappear along with the blood and water, longing to be buried in the dark earth, too. But only for a moment.

His last words hang over her, *Woman, here is your son*, as a burning mist. With these words in her heart, she goes to bed. She can still smell Jesus on the folded bloodied clothing nearby, as well as the oils from the burial preparation. Holding these in her heart, she closes her eyes on this most horrifying day. Her last thoughts before sleep are of the Passover hymns and her love for her son.

On the morning of Easter, though she would not call it that, Mary awakes to an aroma—something sweet and clean and pure, the most delightful fragrance she has ever smelled. *What is that?* she wonders. She rises slowly and walks to the window. Looking out, her heart catches. The young tree on which she poured the water and her son's blood is covered in brilliant, fresh white blossoms. It is the aroma coming from these blossoms that awakened her. It is a pure, glorious scent, like fine incense.

And then, in that moment, she feels him behind her. She turns to see Jesus standing before her. He is beaming, dressed in dazzling white—and oh, those eyes: the eyes she first saw that night so long ago when he was born and Magi came with gifts and adoration, the eyes that looked down upon her from the cross in agony and intimacy. And now those pure, sweet eyes look on her once more, with all the power of the universe and the eternal God in them, and she knows instantly that he sees all things. She was the first to meet his gaze in life, the last to meet his gaze in death, and now the first to meet his gaze in this new resurrected life.

And Mary knows, too, that, as his kingdom has come to fruition, hers has expanded as well. She drops to her knees, crying, "Lord! Lord, I knew it. I knew you would come!" She can barely raise her eyes to meet his, but as she does, she shuts them tightly, trying to store up his look forever: this living, resurrected, eternal look.

Jesus stretches his arms out to her, and she starts to laugh and cry. They stay this way together a long while, resting in each other's joy. He tells her of many things that he saw in his descent, that mysterious hidden time between his death and resurrection. Then he speaks of her mission, the work he has for her.

That was the scene in my imagination, praying with the idea that Jesus appeared first to his mother after his resurrection. Considering this word—"Woman, here is your son." . . . "Here is your mother"—why do I tell this Easter morning story?

I think it helped me understand two things. First, when Jesus placed Mary in the care of John, he didn't sever a family tie; rather, he reordered a relationship and expanded it. He did not dismiss Mary as his mother but gave her as spiritual mother to the entire burgeoning Church.

And how the Church would need her. It needed her in those early days, filled with fear, persecution, confusion, and so many important decisions to be made. And we need her today.

When Jesus addresses John with "Here is your mother," he is speaking to us, too, inviting us to bring Mary into our home or, as Pope Benedict suggests, to receive her into our inner life.[25] She is with all who carry on the mission. If you struggle in your relationship with Mary, ask yourself how your day might change if you were to take her into your home? Into your daily life? If Mary's primary role is to bring others to Jesus and Jesus to others, how do you share in that work? Are you allowing Mary to show you the way to do that?

The second point I'd like to make concerning my meditation about Easter morning is that it's often during times of suffering that our role, perhaps even our vocation, is refined or defined. This is what happened for Mary when, in her anguish, she stood at the foot of the cross. There she entered into her son's suffering, making it her own, sharing in it. In that moment, as her heart expanded through sorrow, the Lord established her influence in the Church in a unique way.

Jesus often moves things around inside us during a period of suffering. That process can affect our vocation, expanding or contracting or even defining it for the first time. Perhaps in suffering, our hearts are open in a particular way, freer to respond to his prompting, especially when we stay close to Jesus, joining our suffering to his.

I often tell directees who are suffering something especially difficult to look for markers around their vocation: Is this suffering redefining their vocation in some way? Is

"

Jesus often moves things around inside us during a period of suffering. Perhaps in suffering, our hearts are open in a particular way, freer to respond to his prompting, especially when we stay close to Jesus, joining our suffering to his.

their assignment in the Church—what God is calling them to do—shifting?

We want to pay attention during periods of suffering to this question: what assignment is Jesus now giving me? He expanded his mother's role at the foot of the cross; is he expanding mine, too?

Her Majesty, Your Majesty

In the early years of my reversion to the Catholic faith, I struggled in my relationship with Mary. I didn't know exactly where to put her or how to address her. Was she an unnecessary distraction from Jesus?

I discovered that to understand Mary, I had to understand womanhood in a proper sense. I needed to embrace the particular gifts that women bring to the Church. Edith Stein is often attributed with saying "The world doesn't need what women have, it needs what woman are." She argued that when a woman enters an environment, she humanizes it. She writes, "Woman naturally seeks to embrace that which is living, personal, and whole. To cherish, guard, protect, nourish and advance growth is her natural, maternal yearning."[26] Pope St. John Paul II and others have spoken of this attribute as entrustment. In the pope's apostolic letter *On the Dignity and Vocation of Women,* he wrote, "The moral and spiritual strength of a woman is joined to her awareness that *God entrusts the human being to her in a special way*."[27] He continued later:

In our own time, the successes of science and technology make it possible to attain material well-being to a degree hitherto unknown. While this favors some, it pushes others to the edges of society. In this way, unilateral progress can also lead to a gradual *loss of sensitivity for man, that is, for what is essentially human.* In this sense, our time in particular *awaits the manifestation* of that "genius" which belongs to women, and which can ensure sensitivity for human beings in every circumstance: because they are human![28]

And of course, no one possessed this attribute of entrustment more powerfully or perfectly than Mary. We can look to Jesus' interaction with his mother—he was mothered, after all—to teach us something about the importance of this gift and how the Church simply cannot flourish without it. The Church needs holy women who understand this gift and are eager to develop and steward it in its many iterations on behalf of the world, which needs it as never before.

Keep in mind that Mary's mothering was hidden, behind the scenes, and it is mostly unknown to us. How many mothers feel that way about their mothering? No one knows how much you really do, what it takes to be a good mother. You're in good company. (Joseph's fathering was also hidden, but we'll save that for another book.)

When we look at Scripture as a whole, we see that right from the start, the Creator links women with guarding the living, with being keepers of life. We read in Genesis:

To the woman he said,

"I will greatly increase your pangs in childbearing [oh,
fabulous!]; . . .
yet your desire shall be for your husband,
     and he shall rule over you" [terrific].

And to the man he said,

"By the sweat of your face
     you shall eat bread
until you return to the ground,
     for out of it you were taken;
you are dust,
     and to dust you shall return." (Genesis 3:16-17, 19).

Thank you, Adam and Eve, for this spectacular inheritance:
sweat, dominance, pain, and dust. But immediately following
God's judgment, "The man named his wife Eve, because she
was the mother of all living" (Genesis 3:20). How interesting.
She who has joined herself to death—who has chosen death
by taking the fruit forbidden by God—shall be called "the
mother of all living." What could God be up to?

Joseph Ratzinger comments on this point in *Daughter Zion:
Meditations on the Church's Marian Beliefs*:

[S]he is the mother of all life, whence she receives her name. In
my opinion it is significant that her name is bestowed in Genesis
3:20 *after* the fall, *after* God's words of judgment. In this way
the undestroyed dignity and majesty of woman are expressed.
She preserves the mystery of life, the power opposed to death;
for death is like the power of nothingness, the antithesis of

Yahweh, who is the creator of life and the God of the living. She, who offers the fruit which leads to death, whose task manifests a mysterious kinship with death, is nonetheless from now on the keeper of the seal of life and the antithesis of death. The woman, who bears the key of life, thus touches directly the mystery of being, the living God, from whom in the last analysis all life originates and who, for that reason, is called "life," the "living one."[29]

Let's pay attention. The dignity of a woman, her majesty, is tied up in her identity as "the keeper of the seal of life," the one "who bears the key of life." Even sin cannot remove this identity. In this way, women touch God's very being: he is the *living* God, the *living* one.

This is pure gift for women. It's not something we've conjured; it's not something we've earned; it's not something we merit. It is gift, something entrusted to us. It is our *entrustment*.

This entrustment of human life to women has deep resonance today, perhaps more than at any other time in history. Abortion, abuse, human trafficking, pornography, addiction, euthanasia—I could go on enumerating the plagues engulfing society. Women, the world needs you—your dignity and majesty. Right here, right now. Never doubt it.

Do Whatever He Tells You

There is one particular interaction between Jesus and his mother that helps illustrate this feminine genius at work: the wedding at Cana.

On the third day there was a wedding in Cana of Galilee, and the mother of Jesus was there. Jesus and his disciples had also been invited to the wedding. When the wine gave out, the mother of Jesus said to him, "They have no wine." And Jesus said to her, "Woman, what concern is that to you and to me? My hour has not yet come." His mother said to the servants, "Do whatever he tells you." Now standing there were six stone water jars for the Jewish rites of purification, each holding twenty or thirty gallons. Jesus said to them, "Fill the jars with water." And they filled them up to the brim. He said to them, "Now draw some out, and take it to the chief steward." So they took it. When the steward tasted the water that had become wine, and did not know where it came from (though the servants who had drawn the water knew), the steward called the bridegroom and said to him, "Everyone serves the good wine first, and then the inferior wine after the guests have become drunk. But you have kept the good wine until now." Jesus did this, the first of his signs, in Cana of Galilee, and revealed his glory; and his disciples believed in him. (John 2:1-11)

This is a very rich passage, and I will highlight a few important points about it before we consider its broader meaning. First, Jesus' presence at the wedding feast signals his sanctification of the covenant of marriage. Second, his use of the title "Woman" was a sign of respect and endearment, not one of disrespect, as it may sound to modern ears. Third, this event takes place on the third day, a clear foreshadowing of Jesus' resurrection on the third day, when his glory is made manifest. And fourth, when Jesus refers to "my hour," he is referencing not only his *historical* hour, his sacrifice on Golgotha, but his *liturgical* hour, too—the sacrament of the Eucharist that we celebrate at every Mass.

But I want to concentrate here on the exchange between Mary and Jesus and in particular the way in which Mary applies her "feminine genius"—her motherhood, her majesty as keeper of life. Yes, she sees the need of the couple. Yes, she probably steps in so as to prevent embarrassment. But there is much more going on here.

In this passage, Mary brings to life the saying "A mother does not prepare a path for her child, but her child for the path." Mary, having prepared Jesus, sends him forth on his path at the wedding feast at Cana. Significantly, she does so with the last words Scripture records from her: "Do whatever he tells you" (John 2:5).

Whereas Eve, in the Fall, invited Adam to sin, Mary, as the new Eve, serves as a corrective to the Fall by inviting Jesus into his messianic mission. She invites her son to step into his fullness. Mary sees who Jesus is, all he is. She sees his bloodline, her bloodline. She sees perhaps the ending of her stewardship of him. Henceforth, he will give her assignments; he will be her judge. She will do whatever he tells her.

In the final analysis, this role as the keeper of life is part of our dignity as women that cannot be destroyed—maimed and corrupted maybe, but never destroyed. I want to suggest that deeply rooted in Mary's role—in *our* role as keepers of the seal of life—is a burning hope in the child. It is a holy confidence in the blessedness of the child, the blessedness of the human person, the dignity of the human person.

Mary waters the roots of the young tree with her son's blood, but it is her blood as well. It is her majesty, her dignity, her feminine courage at its best to trust that the blood—the sacrifice, the toil, the vocation of her son's life—will bring about the greatest good. She hopes in him. She carries with her the fullness of hope in him. It is not human optimism but divine hope.

The world is in desperate need of such strong mothering, of women who understand the importance of their dignity and their gift of entrustment. Women like this will help reclaim what has been lost to a culture of death. Women like this will help the Church and the world flourish and bloom.

PROMPT FOR PRAYER

Fiat at the Foot of the Cross

Prayer Exercise One

Read the following passage several times. As vividly as you can, place yourself in the scene. Remember to see the people, hear the words, observe the action.[30] In particular, pay attention to what Jesus says and does. Stay close to Jesus in your meditation.

> Meanwhile, standing near the cross of Jesus were his mother, and his mother's sister, Mary the wife of Clopas, and Mary Magdalene. When Jesus saw his mother and the disciple whom he loved standing beside her, he said to his mother, "Woman, here is your son." Then he said to the disciple, "Here is your mother." And from that hour the disciple took her into his own home. (John 19:25-27)

Where are you in the scene? Who are you? How do you interact with the Lord? What does he say to you, and what do you say to him?

Prayer Exercise Two

Read the annunciation passage several times:

> In the sixth month the angel Gabriel was sent by God to a town in Galilee called Nazareth, to a virgin engaged to a man whose name was Joseph, of the house of David. The virgin's name was Mary. And he came to her and said, "Greetings, favored one! The Lord is with you." But she was much perplexed by his words and pondered what sort of greeting this might be. The angel said to her, "Do not be afraid, Mary, for you have found favor with God. And now, you will conceive in your womb and bear a son, and you will name him Jesus. He will be great, and will be called the Son of the Most High, and the Lord God will give to him the throne of his ancestor David. He will reign over the house of Jacob forever, and of his kingdom there will be no end." Mary said to the angel, "How can this be, since I am a virgin?" The angel said to her, "The Holy Spirit will come upon you, and the power of the Most High will overshadow you; therefore the child to be born will be holy; he will be called Son of God. And now, your relative Elizabeth in her old age has also conceived a son; and this is the sixth month for her who was said to be barren. For nothing will be impossible with God." Then Mary said, "Here am I, the servant of the Lord; let it be with me according to your word." Then the angel departed from her. (Luke 1:26-38)

What strikes you most about this exchange between Gabriel and Mary? Is there a word or phrase that sticks out for you?

Do you remember a moment in your life when you said yes to the will of the Father? What were the results of that yes?

Is there a current *fiat* before you, an invitation to serve and to build up the kingdom in some new way?

† † †

QUESTIONS FOR DISCUSSION OR JOURNALING

1. Are you in the midst of some particular suffering? When the time is right—perhaps when you can sit quietly before the Lord in the tabernacle—ask, "How is this suffering refining my vocation, my role in the Church?"

2. Can you think of a time when someone suffered with you? What was that experience like? How did their presence affect your own suffering?

3. Has there been a time when you felt called to suffer with another? What was that experience like? What did it teach you? What graces did it bring?

4. Does Mary have a place in the home of your heart? What are some new ways that you could "take Mary into your home"?

CHAPTER 4

The Fourth Word

"My God, my God, why have you forsaken me?"
—Matthew 27:46

I'd just finished giving an online conference on the tricky subject "When Healing Doesn't Happen," when an email from a woman who attended the talk popped into my inbox. She wrote to say she'd been suffering from a serious illness for years. She prays her Rosary, says her novenas, makes holy hours, reads the Bible, and fasts and gives alms in the ways she can. She goes to Mass and Confession when she is able. Still she remains ill. "What am I doing wrong?" she asked.

It's a legitimate question, a human question: Why won't Jesus heal me? rescue me? fix it? What possible good can be gained from my continued suffering?

St. Padre Pio once suggested if we knew the value of suffering, we'd ask for more of it.[31] My friend, I am not able to pray for that yet, but I'm sure the saint is right. Still, *My God, my God, why have you forsaken me?* may be one of the most well-known lamentations in all human history. It is vitally important that we allow it to teach and form our prayer life and our faith.

Jesus' question calls to mind one of my favorite drawings by the great Carmelite master and Doctor of the Church St. John of the Cross; it's probably his most highly recognized drawing. It's a rough sketch of the crucifixion, which in itself is not particularly unusual; St. John was fond of making and drawing crosses. But what is unusual about this sketch is the perspective. John chose to draw it from above. One could suppose it is drawn from the Father's viewpoint, looking down on his Son as he hangs on the cross.[32]

I have often used this drawing to initiate discussion on the crucifixion and the challenging reality that sometimes the Father does not answer our prayers the way we wish. Sometimes our suffering remains.

Let's imagine this depiction of the crucifixion for a moment. Let's view Jesus on the cross as though we are on a platform several feet above him and to his left. We don't see his face, but we can clearly see the top of his head crowned in thorns, the nails protruding from his hands and feet, his body hanging in bitter agony.

Now imagine Jesus calling out, "*Eli, Eli, lema sabachthani?*" Ask yourself, what do I see in this moment? If this is the Father's perspective, his viewpoint, what am I witnessing? Is the Father neglectful? Disinterested? Cruel? Why doesn't he intervene? If he is not rescuing his Son, am I witnessing a lack of power or a deficiency in God Almighty? Does the Father forsake Jesus?

Scholars tell us that when Jesus utters this word, he is referring to the first line of Psalm 22 (or Psalm 21 in the Vulgate) and that to call on one line of a psalm is to recall the psalm in its entirety. And like so many of the psalms that begin with lament, Psalm 22 ends with a celebration of and total confidence in the Father's faithfulness. So this cry of the Lord from the cross isn't a moment of questioning the Father's love but of acknowledging it.

Let's revisit a few lines from Psalm 22:

> My God, my God, why have you forsaken me?
>   Why are you so far from helping me, from the words of my groaning?
> O my God, I cry by day, but you do not answer;
>   and by night, but find no rest.
>
> Yet you are holy,
>   enthroned on the praises of Israel.
> In you our fathers trusted;
>   they trusted, and you delivered them.
> To you they cried, and were saved;
>   in you they trusted, and were not disappointed. (Psalm 22:1-5, RSVCE)

We see here the classic method of the lamentation psalm, beginning with an agonized groan and turning almost instantly into a crescendo of praise for God's faithfulness. The psalmists were not emotionally unstable, capricious, or immature; rather, they were passionate, and they tried to hold together the dynamic tension of human suffering and sin with the greatness and mystery of God. Furthermore, they received the psalms as inspired by God. We can trust, as Carmelite author Fr. Wilfrid Stinissen says, that God himself has given us these prayers.[33]

Again, scholars tell us that this word from the cross is not so much a moment of doubt as a moment of remembrance. Jesus is not questioning the Father's love and care but calling upon it in its fullness, calling on it in light of eternity. He might have just as easily said, "Father, I trust you; you will deliver me!" We could say this word is a gesture forward, a prophetic glance toward the fidelity of God the Father and a fulfillment of his word.

I trust that scholarship. I believe that interpretation is correct. But here I don't want to concentrate on that idea, however helpful it may be for some. Instead, I want to stay within the moment of lamentation. It is such a critically important part of prayer that we don't want to skip over it. It is an equally important part of Christ's prayer. Because he can pray, "Why have you forsaken me?" we know that we can pray those words, too. Because he can ask his Father this question, so can you and I.

And who among the living has not prayed this prayer, wailed within our deepest selves this lamentation? Maybe we were sick and prayed for health, and health didn't come. We were childless and prayed for babies and were met instead with infertility and a too-quiet house. Or we felt so lonely we thought our heart would split in two, and still no one kept us company. We needed work to feed our children and were met with layoffs and an economic downturn. Or perhaps we earnestly sought forgiveness from one we had betrayed, and instead, they closed their heart to us forever.

We ask for good things, normal things, human things. We ask God to address the most common needs, yet sometimes we are met with abject silence. No *yes* or *no*, just nothing. *My God, I have done all that you have asked. I have done the best I knew to do. Why have you forgotten me, when I love you so, when I have tried so hard? Why have you abandoned me to this darkness?* And God remains quiet.

Lamentation is a legitimate season of the human heart. We don't want to assume that we're failing in our faith life if we find ourselves in that season—or if, as we lament, we meet a silent God.

"Where Is Jesus?"

This story came first from a Dominican friend, the poet and writer Fr. Paul Murray, who served as Mother Teresa's spiritual director for a time. His book *I Loved Jesus in the Night* discusses her experience of spiritual darkness, and it includes more details about this story.[34]

During Eucharistic Adoration at a retreat for the Missionaries of Charity in Calcutta, Mother Teresa passed a note to the priest leading the retreat. It read, "Father, please pray for me. Where is Jesus?" I have seen this note with my own eyes, held it in my hand: Mother Teresa's scrawl on a scrap of paper, like a child's handwriting, unsure but trying hard. The priest immediately looked over at Mother Teresa, and she met his gaze. Then she knelt in adoration, turning her eyes to the silent Christ of the Holy Eucharist.

Can you imagine how piercing this moment must have been? Of course, now we know much more of Mother Teresa's experience: her years of spiritual aridity and loneliness. In her private writings, she lamented, "The darkness is so dark, and the pain is so painful. But I accept whatever He gives and I give whatever He takes."[35]

That is a woman supremely surrendered to the will of the One she loves. That is a woman crying out, "In you our fathers trusted . . . and were not disappointed" (Psalm 22:5, 6, NABRE).

This faithful, exceptional woman, who gave her entire life to God and to serving the poorest of the poor, found herself asking, "Where is Jesus?" Surely, we say, she must be one of God's favorites! How is it possible, in what reality does it make any sense, that God would withdraw from her? And if the Lord did withdraw from her, what are my chances that he won't abandon me, who probably deserves abandonment for all my petty sins?

What do we do with this? Where do we go when, to borrow Msgr. Hugh Benson's phrase, "The very reasons for faithfulness appear to vanish"?[36]

A Father Who Does Not Intervene

In my first marriage, which was brief and troubled (and for which the Church granted a declaration of nullity years later), bedtime was one of the most painful parts of the day. I used to lie in bed at night, every night, waiting for my husband to join me. And every night he would linger a long while downstairs after I'd retired. I would pray—groaning from places so deep in my heart that I hadn't known they existed—that my husband might say goodnight, kiss my forehead, touch my hand—anything to indicate that he knew I was there, that he was glad I was there. I longed for him to offer even the smallest point of connection.

But night after night in those nine long months of living under the same roof, my husband would eventually settle into bed without the least acknowledgment of me, of us. This was excruciatingly painful—I'm certain for both of us.

Sometime after our divorce, I was recalling this experience in prayer. I remembered lying in bed, crying out silently to the Lord, begging him to intervene in my marriage. And night after night, I was crushed by our failure to connect. In prayer I asked God, "Jesus, where were you? I was in so much pain; I died every night. Every night I begged your help. Where were you in that?"

An image came to me. I was lying in bed, my husband lying next to me, his back turned to me. I was staring at the ceiling, crying out to the Lord, begging him to intervene. Suddenly he appeared, hovering over me, his arms stretched wide as if to embrace me. If I had raised my hand, I might have touched his face. He was there, looking tenderly at me.

I realized he'd been there all along, hovering over me. I realized, too, that his arms were outstretched because he was on the cross—and he was dying, too.

Just so, this sketch from St. John of the Cross—the crucifixion from the point of view of the Father—suggests that, in fact, God the Father was there when Jesus called to him. The Father was there, watching and witnessing, and he was dying, too.

Fr. Stinissen reminds us that in the Eucharist, the Lord comes to us wounded and sacrificed. And that is the right moment to pray, "Jesus, heal these wounds."

As soon as you show him your wounds and expose yourself to his healing power, the healing process begins, one that is not like ordinary healing. It is not a question of something old that has caused you much pain and finally ceases to torment you. The healing goes back into time and transforms the very moment when you were hurt into a moment of grace. The very wound that was the cause of so much suffering is transformed into a blessing, and all the bitterness it caused is changed into meaningful and fruitful suffering.[37]

When my problems are not resolved, my illnesses not healed, my pains not alleviated, I think of this image of the crucifixion from St. John, and I am in awe of the Father's supreme restraint. What must it have taken for him to *stay* his hand, to *not* intervene in the crucifixion, to be so close to his suffering Son and yet do nothing? This teaches me that the value in our suffering and free will must be unspeakably great for the Father to respect it so perfectly, so profoundly. Indeed, a Father who does not end our suffering, though he certainly could, must see its worth. And it must take all the love in his heart to allow it to continue, so that something glorious and eternal might be achieved in us and through us.

Fr. Vann writes, "You need suffering of one sort or another to become adult in love; you need it to understand the depths of love; . . . you need it in order to experience the deepest truths and realities."[38] In another place, he says, "There is something lacking even to the most brilliant mind until it has deep experience of love, and the way to that is suffering."[39]

When your suffering lingers, you can confidently assume that the Father is up to something good, perhaps even spectacular, in you. Suffering is a unique opportunity to join directly in the work of Jesus on the cross, to atone for our sins and the sins of the world. Our suffering can be a powerful weapon against evil in the world if we put it in the hands of the Lord and let him do with it as he wishes.

From Suffering to Self-Donation

"My God, why have you forsaken me?" We don't want to abuse this prayer, but we needn't fear it. We mustn't wallow; we must run from self-pity as from the plague. We need to see lamentation for what it is, a vehicle to the next phase in the spiritual life, a stepping stone to greater strength, compassion, vision, and—perhaps most important and least appreciated—atonement.

Again, we don't want to abuse this season of the faith life, and we don't want to become trapped within it. Instead, like the psalmist, we want to let it carry us to the next stage in our spiritual progress, to recognition and praise of the Father Almighty—and very often, into service and spiritual works of mercy. This word is ultimately an invitation to give as Jesus gives.

How do the holiest among us do that? How do we acknowledge and accept our suffering without remaining trapped in it or controlled by it? How do we go on to extraordinarily selfless lives of service?

Let's take careful note of this link between spiritual darkness and self-donation. Christ's cry from the cross—"My God, why have you forsaken me?"—is deeply, eternally tied to complete self-donation. Those who choose self-donation are free souls who willingly allow themselves to be taken up in service to God, in whatever form God might ask. They trust that the Father will transform their suffering, redeem their suffering, achieve great things through their suffering. We can do the same.

Too often we think of suffering as something to be endured. We don't take advantage of it. We don't ask God to come in and give it meaning and purpose, to make it redemptive. Even the sick can lead lives of total self-giving. By accepting in love and even gratitude their circumstances, and by allowing those in charge of their care to be sanctified through their work, they unleash powerful graces in the world.

Consider, for example, John Paul II's prolonged suffering with Parkinson's disease, what author George Weigel has so appropriately called "his last encyclical."[40] One of the television movies about the pope depicts a scene just after his diagnosis. He raises a fist to heaven and says something to the effect of "Really? You're going to allow me to be struck down now? When I have so much work to do?"

Who knows if that moment ever took place, but I can imagine it. In that same scene, the pope turns immediately to a priest friend and asks him to hear his confession.

If the pope did have a few moments of lamentation, he didn't stay in them long. He continued to travel worldwide, to write, to lead the Church through challenges of the highest order. As his body was slowly ravaged, how often did he appear before the needy crowds, drooling, bent, and smiling, blessing and loving his flock until his last breath?

Pope St. John Paul II pointed out magnificently, in his life and in his writing, that suffering unleashes love.[41] If suffering

"

Too often we think of
suffering as something to be
endured. We don't take
advantage of it. We don't
ask God to come in and give
it meaning and purpose,
to make it redemptive.

had a vocation, it would be this: to unleash love in the world. There can be no greater service than this.

But suffering is hard. It hurts, and the temptation is to withdraw, to hold back, to guard our hearts, to imagine that we've done all we promised, but God has not kept up his end of the bargain. Who needs it? Let's turn on the television and check out.

We return to Mother Teresa. We know now how dark the last half of her life was; the absolute absence of God pierced her inexplicably, privately, silently. "Where is Jesus?" She seemed to live in a permanent state of divine abandonment. In light of all this, how can we account for her extraordinary life of service? In her prolonged period of divine abandonment, what did she do?

Yes, Mother asked, "Where is Jesus?" But then she poured herself even more fervently into service. "Let Him do with me whatever He wants. . . . If my darkness is light to some souls . . . I am perfectly happy," she wrote.[42] Did this end her aridity? Her divine loneliness? Apparently not. But does anyone question her choice?

Does anyone reading about her life doubt that she made the right choice in continuing to serve the poorest of the poor despite her suffering? Who would argue that she should have packed her bags and moved to Bermuda? Mother Teresa accepted *what* he gave and *what* he took and then went out in *service*.

It seems exceedingly clear, when we examine Christ on the cross and the lives of saints like Mother Teresa and John Paul II, that they would not linger in lamentation but would allow it to carry them like a wave into powerful, meaningful service. When I find myself tempted to wallow in lamentation—on the truly rare occasions when all the reasons for faithfulness seem to have vanished—I hope I can follow my lament with "Yet you are holy! How may I serve you? Lord, let me serve you. Through this darkness, through this suffering, through this utter abandonment, O Jesus, may I serve you."

Ultimately, of course, we see this in Jesus. His prayer in the garden was *Not my will but yours be done* (Luke 22:42). And hours later, while he was hanging on the cross, his lamentation was real: "My God, why have you abandoned me?" Then he died in service, in total self-donation.

Part of the Plot

In our suffering—especially at its worst, its most prolonged, its most mystifying—we can follow the example of Christ. We can begin where he begins. We can pray as he prays. We can make his words our words.

You are an essential part of the story of salvation; you have a unique role to play. Keep in mind that the life of a Christian is never a tragedy. It may occasionally be a thriller or a mystery, but it will end up being a love story, your love story with the Lord. Lamentation and suffering are just part of the plot.

Be free to cry out with all your heart in lamentation, but trust that the Lord is right there, suffering with you, hovering close by. You are not alone, and he is not indifferent to your pain. Then keep moving, allowing that lamentation to carry you into purer works of service and mercy. And never forget to end a day of suffering with sincere praise. Allow the Lord to swallow up your lamentation with his faithfulness.

If you find yourself in a season of lamentation, stay with this word from Jesus on the cross. As Fr. Stinissen writes, "[Jesus] wants us to share in his own happiness, which is the happiness of giving."[43] Lament as you will, and then move on to give as Jesus gives.

PROMPT FOR PRAYER

Praying with the Psalms: You Were Made for Praise

The psalms hold a unique place in the heart of the praying Church. They serve a pivotal role in the daily office prayed by priests and religious as well as lay men and women, including my ninety-four-year-old father. Their breadth, depth, and personal quality make them particularly helpful in teaching us to pray.

It can be no surprise that the psalms make their presence felt even at the crucifixion. Jesus would have known them intimately and would have prayed them his whole life.

Thomas Merton wrote:

The Psalms are not only the revealed word of God, not only the words which God Himself has indicated to be those which He likes to hear from us. . . . The words and thoughts of the Psalms spring not only from the unsearchable depths of God, but also from the inmost heart of the Church, and there are no songs which better express her soul, her desires, her longing, her sorrows, and her joys.[44]

Fr. Stinissen reminds us, "There is a wonderful dosage of lamentation and praise in the Psalms with a noticeable balance on the side of praise. We are not created to lament but to praise."[45] We do well to pay extra attention to them in our prayers, to adopt them as the song of our heart and soul.

Choose one of the following psalms according to your current needs, and pray with it for a few minutes. Read it several times, slowly, while paying attention to the phrases or stanzas that capture your heart and imagination. After praying with the psalm for some time, choose the most meaningful stanzas and rewrite them in your own words, personalizing them. Ask the Holy Spirit to guide you.

Remember to finish with praise. Thank the Lord for moments in your life when he has demonstrated his love for you.

Psalms to Turn to:

When you need healing:
　† Psalm 38: "I am utterly spent and crushed" (verse 8).

When you need patience:
　† Psalm 130: "I wait for the LORD, my soul waits, and in his word I hope" (verse 5).

When you need to remember who God Almighty is:
　† Psalm 22: "Yet you are holy" (verse 3).
　† Psalm 104: "O LORD, my God, you are very great" (verse 1).

When you are suffering persecution:

    † Psalm 13: "How long, O LORD, Will you forget me forever?" (verse 1).

    † Psalm 69: "I sink in deep mire" (verse 2).

    † Psalm 3: "How many are my foes!" (verse 1).

When you need mercy:

    † Psalm 51: "Create in me a clean heart" (verse 10).

When you want to say thank you:

    † Psalm 92: "It is good to give thanks to the LORD" (verse 1).

    † Psalm 138: "I give you thanks, O LORD, with my whole heart" (verse 1).

    † Psalm 147: "He heals the brokenhearted" (verse 3).

† † †

QUESTIONS FOR DISCUSSION OR JOURNALING

1. Name some concrete gifts that have come to you through your suffering. What was the circumstance of your suffering, and how did those gifts come to you through it?

2. Are you thinking about lamentation and the psalms in a new way? How?

3. Do you have a favorite psalm? What draws you to that particular psalm?

4. If they are not already a part of your prayer, what's one way you could add the psalms to your daily reflections?

CHAPTER 5

The Fifth Word

"I thirst."
—*John 19:28, RSVCE*

A woman approached me after a retreat I'd led and told me her story.

After nearly ten years of sobriety, this woman had relapsed in a dramatic fashion. During this time, and in some part due to her drug-induced negligence, her teenage daughter was kidnapped and trafficked. In an extraordinary turn of events, some months later the authorities found the girl and brought her home. She now lives in an institution, where she battles for her life and her sanity. The horrors of the daughter's experience were such that it's unclear whether she will be able to live outside an institution again.

The mother has broken free of drugs and alcohol once again, and she is fighting like a lioness, doing everything she can for this daughter who was miraculously returned to her. Still, the grief, the regret: she wears them like a heavy wet coat three sizes too big. There are no easy amends here. She asked me, "How can I ever forgive myself?"

In that moment I thought, *There it is: that still, small voice that says, "I thirst."*

Another woman, on another retreat, told me that her husband had died not long before of a merciless, progressive, degenerative illness. Caring for him, watching him suffer this way over years, she said, nearly killed her. And it turned out that the disease is genetic and was passed on to her eldest son. Now dying in this merciless manner, he is angry and bitter, thrashing out at the world around him—including his mother—for his cruel fate.

As this woman sat with me, I noticed how slight she was: maybe a hundred pounds, like a little sack of frail bones. And so weary. "I don't know if I can do this again," she said, and I believed her.

Once more, there it was, so faint you'd miss it if you didn't pay attention: *I thirst.*

Another soul, I learned on another retreat, had recently lost her very young grandchildren and daughter-in-law to murder-suicide. No one saw it coming. There was no history of mental illness. No one even knew there was a gun in the house. "How can God be God?" this woman wondered earnestly. No bitterness had yet made its way into her heart, only the agony of the impossibility that this tragedy would ever make sense.

I listened to this grandmother, hard and long, as she explained how she would never be whole again, "not on this side of heaven." I strained my ears to hear—so low, so faint—but here, too, Jesus whispered, *I thirst.*

You don't have to look far to know that life can be unspeakably cruel. Even with its joys and mysteries, it's precarious. Life can be so easily overturned, overwhelmed in an instant by unquenchable soul thirsts: for justice, for relief, for answers.

But perhaps more than any other word of Jesus from the cross, "I thirst" presents an opportunity to see that Jesus' choice to take on human nature—and all that implies—is a supreme act of compassion. To hear Jesus say, "I thirst" may not help to end your suffering, but it crushes to dust the lie that you are isolated from the Lord in your suffering. In the most profound way possible, it proves Jesus is right there with you, in it. And he's not going anywhere.

A Truly Human God

Many years ago, as I was developing a habit of late-night Adoration at a chapel, I started throwing kisses to the tabernacle on arrival and departure. I don't know why I started it; I just felt compelled. If I could have hugged the tabernacle or the monstrance, I might have. I suppose I just wanted to express my affection.

Kneeling and bowing are wonderful expressions of reverence, deeply meaningful, but a kiss is more intimate, more personal. A priest once told me that the heart in love wants to vow itself, and I suppose the heart in love wants to express affection, too. So I throw Jesus kisses.

It's a tiny gesture. I do it privately, in a hidden kind of way. Somewhere in the back of my mind, I think of that kiss of Judas, that cruelest kiss. I'd like to think that my small gesture might help heal that wound.

Years after I'd begun this devotion, I had the opportunity to go on retreat abroad with a priest who has received the stigmata and other supernatural gifts. A retreat with him had been described as akin to sitting at the feet of Jesus for a week. It was an apt description. I quickly forgot about the supernatural phenomena that visited him; his teaching and wisdom mesmerized me. I didn't want his talks to end. As long as they were—hours sometimes—I never seemed to get tired.

Our week unfolded according to a pattern: the priest would teach us in the morning, we'd have homework for the afternoon, and in the evening, we'd have Mass together. At Mass, after Communion, the priest would guide us through meditations. There would be about fifty of us in a fairly small room in a modest retreat center, so every chair would be taken. The priest and his interpreter sat in the front at a table, facing all of us.

During one service, we had our heads bowed as he talked us through the meditation. For whatever reason, I felt compelled to look up. When I did, I was surprised to find the priest was looking directly at me and smiling. I smiled back, and just like that, he threw me a kiss. I blushed and was filled with delight.

I thought I might have imagined it, but later I asked his interpreter if she'd seen it, and she said yes. In all the years she had worked with him, she had never seen him throw anyone a kiss.

The first time I went to Adoration after returning home, I threw a kiss to the Blessed Sacrament as I was leaving. Suddenly it seemed as if all the lights went on, all at once, inside a dark room. I started giggling as I realized that every little gesture of affection I have expressed toward the Lord has been noted: every glance during the day to say thank you or to tell him I love him or how grateful I am for my life; every kiss I have thrown toward the tabernacle; every bit of affection and reverence I have expressed. He has seen and received it all.

Why do I like this story? What does it tell me about Jesus? That he took on human nature. He was *human.*

Jesus could have come as an angel with an angelic nature or as a burning bush and booming voice or in some other way that would have separated him from our bodily vulnerability. But he chose to become human. He subjected himself to the laws of human nature—learning to walk, talk, and work. He had human needs and human responses to human situations. He knew what it meant to have a human body that experiences vulnerability, pain and suffering, hunger and thirst. He understands the human need for love and friendship. He took on a body that housed a soul—just like you and me.

And because Jesus took on human nature—that weird, mysterious composite of body and soul—all of human nature is exalted. You, in your humanity, because of the Incarnation, are exalted. This means your body matters, your needs matter, your humanity matters. They are not arbitrary, insignificant, or random.

Theologian Fr. Roch Kereszty explained:

In Christ human nature has reached its highest, freely bestowed actualization as the human nature of the eternal Son. This has radically changed not only the situation but also the concrete nature of every human being. Because of the incarnation, to be a man or woman means to be a brother or sister of God the Son and *to have a right to be loved by him* as his own brother or sister.[46]

Can we take in the fullness of this claim? How would your day change if you walked through the world embodying your right to be loved by the Lord?

We need to extend the reality of this miracle to everyone—the whole world, even those who hate us and persecute us. Fr. Kereszty continues, "For each one of us to relate to and to love another human being means to relate to and to love a brother or sister of God the Son."[47] Which is another way of saying: Jesus has made humanity holy. He has made our nature one that deserves great reverence—no matter how well actualized that human nature might be or might not be in a person.

This knowledge should act like our first breath in the morning. It must inform every act of mercy, every act of helping, every moment of compassion. And what's more, it should settle our hearts in the deep, holy knowledge that Jesus desires an intimate friendship with each of us.

Called to Compassion

We would do well to remind ourselves what compassion actually is. Spiritual director and counselor Sr. Margaret Ferris wrote that the Latin expression for compassion, *cumpatior*, means "to stand *with*, to undergo *with*, to share deeply *with*." Compassion does not place a protective barrier between me and another; compassion places me inside another's experience. She goes on—and let's pay attention here:

Compassion is not pity which sometimes connotes condescension. No, there is a mutuality about compassion which carries with it *a recognition of the other as holy.* Moreover, compassion does not end at the feeling level but moves outward toward the alleviation of a suffering or the celebration of a joy.[48]

Compassion first and foremost means to "share with," to enter into the suffering or joy of another. Then compassion moves us to take action: working to alleviate suffering, for example. But first we enter into the other's experience.

We get that turned around sometimes, I think. I don't want others to suffer. I want their suffering to end. I'm happy to give a few bucks to the beggar at the stop sign who's just trying to feed himself that day. I'm happy to ask his name and tell him mine, and that's not nothing. But I certainly cannot claim that that is truly entering into his suffering and standing with him in it.

That is precisely what compassion means, and it is what Jesus wanted to do for us: to stand with us in the fullness of our humanity. In doing so, humanity is made holy. You, my friend, are holy territory. This is why Jesus' adopting human nature is a supreme act of compassion: this is how he could stand with us, to share himself most deeply with us, to enter into our suffering, to share our joys. Pope Benedict XVI wrote,

> Jesus has to enter into the drama of human existence, for that belongs to the core of his mission; he has to penetrate it completely, down to its uttermost depths, in order to find the "lost sheep," to bear it on his shoulders, and to bring it home.[49]

"

Because Jesus can stand
with you in your suffering,
you can stand—and must
stand, in the ways that you
are able—with others.

It wasn't enough for Jesus to speak to us, to teach us, to give us his wisdom, to share his divine mind. He desired a much more significant intimacy. He would stand with us in our suffering, entering into it willingly.

This is a great testimony to the deepest desires of God's heart. He wants to stand with his creation and to share deeply the fullness of their experience of life, even their suffering. That he honors us in this way should leave us speechless.

But there's more. "I thirst," Jesus says from the cross. Because Jesus can stand with you in your suffering, you can stand—and must stand, in the ways that you are able—with others.

I'm sure you've had this experience: when something happens to one human, in a way we feel it happens to all of us. Because we share a nature, a beingness.

I think of September 11, 2001, the day the Twin Towers of the World Trade Center were attacked in New York City. I was sitting at my desk at Dartmouth College, emailing back and forth with a colleague. I was complaining about how someone had been rude to me that morning, when suddenly he interrupted our exchange to say, "A plane just struck one of the Twin Towers!"

I immediately jumped onto a news website and sat there, stunned, as that dreadful day began to unfold. When the second plane hit, it was as if the whole world felt the impact. Even if we didn't know anyone on those planes or in those buildings, we felt the terror unleashed in New York, at the Pentagon, and in the Pennsylvania countryside. The human nature we share allowed us to stand with and to share deeply with all those who were attacked that day.

"Mama, I'm So Lonely"

When Jesus says, "I thirst," he expresses human need. And in doing so, he affirms the fact that he has taken on human nature so that he may stand with us—so that he may stand with *you* in your joys and in your sufferings. When we invite Jesus into our sufferings, they can become powerful points of conversion.

One instance many years ago made this crystal clear to me. I was preparing to speak at a women's conference on relationships and how we can strengthen our Christian friendships. About two days before my talk, I had a strong sense that I should include a section on loneliness. I had been working on the issue of loneliness for some time, and though the topic didn't perfectly align with my talk, I couldn't escape the idea that I should speak about it.

I confess that I struggled with terrible loneliness up until the age of forty. Two decades of it at least. It was a radical soul-thirst that I wouldn't wish on my worst enemy. Some of you know what I'm talking about. It can be an unrelenting cross.

By the time of this conference, however, I was on the other side of it. As I got older, the loneliness lifted for a host of reasons, and I no longer carried this burden. Yet I remembered its weight with great clarity. To this day I can sometimes sense when someone else is experiencing it. Ironically, loneliness builds a strange kinship between those who suffer with it.

When the day of the conference arrived, I continued to have a strong sense that I was supposed to include a section on loneliness in my talk, in particular on the gifts that loneliness brings. Over the years, for example, I had come to understand that loneliness was an invitation to enter into Christ's loneliness, to keep him company there. It was an honor to be entrusted with his loneliness in this way.

And so I included this section in my presentation. I gave the same talk three times, to three different groups of women. At the end of my second presentation, one woman came up to me, arms outstretched, crying. She asked, "Can I hug you?"

I said, "Sure," and she collapsed into my arms for a moment, then pulled herself back. She almost couldn't get her next words out. She said, "My boy has autism," and she leaned in again, weeping.

I just held her. When she pulled back a second time, she said, "The other day, he came to me, and he said 'Mama, I'm so lonely.'" She added, "I didn't know how to speak to him about his loneliness until today. You gave me the words to speak to him."

I will never forget that moment: the joy that went through me, the sense of surrender and awe. Interiorly I was flooded with my own little Magnificat: "Your will be done, O Lord! If this is what it takes to help a child who is lonely, so be it. Send me more years of loneliness." Every molecule of loneliness I had suffered was redeemed and restored, transformed into pure gift.

This is one of the ways that Jesus stands with us and heals us: not by relieving us of our pain and suffering, but by joining us in it and then giving it meaning, purpose, a place to go and be used and transformed into heaven's joy. We embody this message when we stand with others.

This is one of the great graces that flow from this word of Christ on the cross, "I thirst." He aligns himself to humanity in a profound way—to all of us who suffer, whose healing does not come though we pray for it, whose bodily demands and emotional ailments cause us suffering and difficulty. "I thirst." Here Jesus tells us—in plain humane terms—"My daughter, my son, I know. I know your pain. I am with you in your pain. I thirst, too. Give me your thirst, that I may quench it with eternal, life-giving water."

Fr. Vann writes,

> The saint must share Christ's suffering. . . . It is the nature of love. But also we are a family; we are each responsible for all. Your suffering is meant to be redemptive, but not for yourself merely but for the world. . . . The pain of Christ is redemptive for all humanity, to bring to all humanity the gifts of understanding and love and sorrow; and you can share by your own pain (and if you love Christ enough you will be impelled to share) in that universality.[50]

Where do you thirst? In body, mind, or spirit? All three? Can you offer this thirst to the Lord? Can you trust him with it, even as he trusts us with his thirst from the cross?

Let's remember that Jesus has taken on human nature so that he can stand with us—in body, heart, mind, and soul. And when you thirst for relief, righteousness, or justice, the Lord is there, thirsting with you, for you, through you.

PROMPT FOR PRAYER

A Compassionate Thirst

As vividly as you can, recreate this moment of Jesus' thirst on the cross. Pray with this passage: "After this Jesus, knowing that all was now finished, said (to fulfil the scripture), 'I thirst'" (John 19:28, RSVCE).

As you pray, imagine that you are standing near the foot of the cross, and you can see Jesus' face. You can hear him say, "I thirst." Allow him to look on you from this place. What does he say to you? What would you like to say to him?

Additional Verses for Prayer

Choose any one of the following verses. Rest with it. Place yourself as vividly as you can in this word.

When your heart is settled, probe these questions: Where do you experience deep soul-thirst in your life? Can you bring this thirst to Jesus? What would it mean for you to pour your thirst into the thirst of Jesus on the cross?

† "Blessed are those who hunger and thirst for righteousness, for they will be filled" (Matthew 5:6).

† Jesus stood up and exclaimed, "Let anyone who thirsts come to me and drink" (John 7:37, NABRE).

† O God, you are my God, I seek you,
    my soul thirsts for you;
  my flesh faints for you,
    as in a dry and weary land where there is no water.
  So I have looked upon you in the sanctuary,
    beholding your power and glory.
  Because your steadfast love is better than life,
    my lips will praise you.
  So I will bless you as long as I live;
    I will lift up my hands and call on your name. (Psalm 63:1-4)

† † †

QUESTIONS FOR DISCUSSION OR JOURNALING

1. You are "fearfully and wonderfully made" (Psalm 139:14). Can you recall a time when you learned something important through your body? For example, the birth of a child, suffering an illness or injury, or enjoying a satisfying, memorable meal?

2. After reading this chapter, are you thinking differently about what it means to be compassionate? In what ways?

3. Is there an area of your life in which you sense the Lord asking you to stand with another? How can you respond to his call?

CHAPTER 6

The Sixth Word

"It is finished."
—John 19:30

It was our last full day in Galilee, and the small group I'd been traveling with gathered for Mass on the Mount of Beatitudes. We were seated before one of the many outdoor altars there, bowing our heads and seeking the presence of the Lord beneath the ancient trees. It was a glorious May Day. The sky was azure, a lovely breeze blew, and off in the distance, sunbeams danced on Lake Gennesaret. It was heavenly.

In that moment, in that setting, praying near where the crowds had gathered to hear Jesus teach, where the beatitudes are fixed in stone as a memorial of the Sermon on the Mount, it can be no wonder that the Spirit would decide to move in a brilliant, culminating way.

Following the Mass, while we were still at prayer, the priest began to lead us through a long, thorough prayer of forgiveness. Slowly, thoughtfully, in the quiet of our hearts, we sincerely asked forgiveness for our sins, and we offered forgiveness where it was needed. People wept openly, and a new lightness seemed to move through us, one by one.

Given that it was only a few months after my divorce had been finalized, my ex-husband was very much on my mind and in my heart. As we moved through the exercises of forgiveness, I discovered that it was much easier to forgive him than it was to forgive myself. Harboring unforgiveness in any form, whether directed at others or directed at ourselves, is a corrosive poison, like a toxin in the blood eating you from the inside out. In that time of prayer, it was as if Jesus gently drained unforgiveness from my bloodstream. And in its place, he infused me with his own precious life-giving blood. I was being reborn in mercy.

Afterward, the priest, who had a charism of healing, offered to pray over us individually. People began to line up on the grass, and the priest, dressed in a crisp white alb, began moving from person to person. At one point, I looked up to see the priest praying over a gentleman in line. He turned in such a way that I could see his face clearly. Only it wasn't the priest I saw; it was my ex-husband! He was beaming and so happy.

It seemed, in that moment, that my ex-husband was there, moving from person to person, placing his hands on their heads in blessing, praying powerful and ancient prayers of deliverance, calling on the holy name of Jesus. He was helping heal and free the souls before him.

This is difficult to describe, except to say this: I think that Jesus was giving me a glimpse of my ex-husband as he would be in heaven. I was seeing him with eternal eyes, seeing him the way the Father—who sees through all time, beyond all time—was seeing him. Clearly the Father was delighting in him, collaborating with him. And this glimpse from the Holy Spirit filled me with indescribable joy.

My ex-husband was *free*. It's not that his life had been all suffering by any means: he was an extraordinary man who had helped countless others. But all the woundedness, every anxiety that had ever plagued him, every emotional issue that had held him prisoner, was washed away. Now he was as he was meant to be, and he was doing God's work, ministering to people. I was particularly struck by his joy and peace.

I knew in my heart that this version of my ex-husband, this fulfillment and perfection of who he was, existed already in the mystery that is eternity. The love I had for him took on a new, purer dimension as a result. "Seeing him" in this way filled me with delight and freed me, too.

Some years passed, and I learned that my ex-husband had been diagnosed with a very aggressive cancer of the blood. He had a month or so to live. I wrote to him right away and offered my support. He wrote back and asked for my prayers. It was a small exchange, but earnest, and I was grateful for it.

Many friends came to me at that time with their prayers and affection, worried that I would be grieving the loss of this man yet again. It was another mourning, certainly, but it was also strangely joyful—because of my glimpse of him on that pilgrimage. I'd had a peek of what awaited him; I had no anxiety or sorrow for him. I mourned for his relatives and closest friends, but for him, I knew, there was freedom ahead, so much joy, and the chance to be who he was created to be in fullness and perfection, forever, with the Father.

I knew my ex-husband had longed for and believed in this fulfillment his whole life. When I pray with this word, "It is finished," I think of him completely free, healed, and whole in heaven.

And when I struggle in painful relationships, I pray with this word. I try to imagine for everyone involved—including me—healing, completion, perfection. In short, I imagine myself and the person before me with all the perfection accomplished through the blood of Jesus outpoured on Golgotha. This is the beatific reality: the ultimate happiness of a direct perception of God in heaven. I try to imagine even enemies standing with me, shoulder to shoulder, worshipping the Lord for eternity.

Gazing upon the crucified Christ, listening to this word, "It is finished," we witness torment, the final surrender. Yet we have confidence that Jesus—living and whole, glorified in heaven—is present on that cross too. We look into his suffering face and see there his resurrected face. A glorified Christ is difficult to see on the cross—difficult to imagine in this bloody, horrifying moment—but that doesn't mean he isn't there.

Consummatum est. "It is accomplished." What feels like a moment of defeat calls for an infusion of beatific blood. We need heaven's help to see Jesus there and to believe—in *this* moment, in *this* word—that perfect glory hangs from bitter wood.

Leaving It All on the Course

My brothers were accomplished triathletes, especially my older brother. At one point, he qualified for world competitions. A ridiculously generous guy, he bought me my first road bike when I was thirty-five.

I fell in love with cycling and eventually competed in my own events—mini-triathlons, as they were called. I remember those days with enormous gratitude. When I see someone biking or running past me, agile and strong, I smile and think, "I used to be able to do that!" I remember how wonderful that felt, and I thank the Lord for so many strong-bodied years.

As I was preparing for my first mini-tri, my brother coached me a bit. He encouraged me with this slogan, common among triathletes: "Leave it all on the course." In other words, leave no hidden pocket of energy, give everything you've got, have no regret once you've crossed the finish line that you might have given even a little bit more.

It was a phrase I later adapted to my Lenten practices; that is, no matter how poorly I may have practiced Lenten disciplines early in the season, by Holy Week I could rededicate myself. There was still time to fast and pray, to finish strong, to leave it all on the course.

Triathlons have not been a part of my life for some time. This tired body wrestles with MS fatigue these days, but I still cling to the notion that I can offer everything I have left to the Lord. In these later years of my life, I don't want to be stingy in stewarding the gifts he has given me. I want to spend them, exhaust them to the end.

I want to leave no little pocket of sin or potential untouched by the light of the Lord. I pray daily that he anoint my potential and touch my faculties so that I do his will, so that he is revealed in and through my life. I want to enter heaven

"

I want to enter heaven completely empty-handed, clinging to no undone work of charity or mercy. I want to be able to say, like the Lord, "It is finished. Father, I've done all you've asked me to do."

completely empty-handed, clinging to no undone work of charity or mercy. I want to be able to say, like the Lord, "It is finished. Father, I've done all you've asked me to do."

I've begun to trust in a new way the Lord's call for us to hold many seeming opposites in dramatic tension: a God who is man, a virgin who is mother, gaining life by losing it. I may not understand these perfectly, but they're not contradictions, not absurdities. Rather, they are paradoxes of the most mystical kind. They reveal God's power, authority, majesty, and, most of all, his love. I can stand before him a sinner but always a sinner who is forgiven again and again and loved to the end.

The Father wants us to know him in these ways. It seems the Lord is always inviting us to embrace paradoxical relationships so that we might relish his mystery and blessedness even more, that we might live in his mystery with joy and trust.

Forgive me this comparison, but the beatitudes are a more elegant way of Jesus telling us to leave it all on the course. They call us to join him in heaven empty-handed and spent, to gain our life by losing it. They ask us to rest in an additional paradoxical truth: that somehow, in an eternal reality, beatitude already *is*. We might witness suffering, but if we look with the right kind of eyes, we'll see the victory, too. All has been accomplished.

In the blessedness of heaven, meekness guards our inheritance, mourning assures our joy, a hunger and thirst for righteousness keeps its promise that we'll never long for justice and decency again. Poverty of heart hands us the keys to the kingdom, and mercy runs wild and in every direction. As I strive to be a peacemaker, the Father himself is claiming me. He is drawing me to himself, to his heart. I belong to him. Here. Now.

Yet it is not unreasonable to ask: Is beatitude just a dream, a cheap spiritual anesthetic? Am I fooling myself through some mental or psychological maneuver that allows me to cope with a world cloaked in sin and darkness? Are the beatitudes the spiritual equivalent of a bumper sticker: "No pain, no gain"? Don't we have to wait for the beatific vision? Can we taste beatitude here and now?

The Womb of the World

No doubt it was another beautiful day in Galilee when Jesus saw the crowd gathering. His heart was moved by their longing, their need, their desire to be near him and to know him. So he situated himself where everyone could catch a glimpse of him and began to teach.

Let's read Matthew's account slowly:

When Jesus saw the crowds, he went up the mountain; and after he sat down, his disciples came to him. Then he began to speak, and taught them, saying:

"Blessed are the poor in spirit, for theirs is the kingdom of heaven.

"Blessed are those who mourn, for they will be comforted.

"Blessed are the meek, for they will inherit the earth.

"Blessed are those who hunger and thirst for righteousness, for they will be filled.

"Blessed are the merciful, for they will receive mercy.

"Blessed are the pure in heart, for they will see God.

"Blessed are the peacemakers, for they will be called children of God.

"Blessed are those who are persecuted for righteousness' sake, for theirs is the kingdom of heaven.

"Blessed are you when people revile you and persecute you and utter all kinds of evil against you falsely on my account. Rejoice and be glad, for your reward is great in heaven, for in the same way they persecuted the prophets who were before you." (Matthew 5:1-12)

Scholars give us different translations of the word *beneditio*, "blessing." Some translations refer to current blessings and others to future or eschatological blessings—that is, those brought to fulfillment in heaven. In a more technical sense, and a sense we do not want to ignore, the beatitudes in Matthew's Gospel refer to this future heavenly blessing.

And yet many of the great minds of the Church argue that "beatitude" is not only a promise for the future. Holy Scripture has its paradoxical tensions. God's word is infinitely expansive yet precise, personal, and universal, speaking to the current moment and to the fullness of time. Pope Benedict wrote,

[The beatitudes] are eschatological promises. This must not, however, be taken to mean that the joy they proclaim is postponed until some infinitely remote future or applies exclusively to the next world. When man begins to see and to live from God's perspective, when he is a companion on Jesus' way, then he lives by new standards, and something of the *éschaton*, of the reality to come [namely heaven], is already present. Jesus brings joy into the midst of affliction.[51]

We might say that Jesus brings heaven to earth, just as he gave me a glimpse of a healed, whole man on the Mount of Beatitudes that day.

Jesus not only keeps his promises, but he gives us new eyes, too. When we ask to see as he sees, to live from his perspective, this is exactly what happens. We begin to see eternity in everything, just as he did. We can think about it in yet another way. This illustration from Peter Kreeft is helpful:

> Earth is not outside heaven; it is heaven's workshop, heaven's womb. . . .
>
> . . . Would it be escapism for a fetus to think about birth? Does life after birth make life in the womb any less important? Doesn't it make it infinitely *more* important? . . .
>
> Heaven is not escapist because we are already there, just as the fetus in the womb is already in the world because the womb is in the world and subject to its laws. . . . We are not yet born from the world-womb, but we are already part of the heavenly Body. . . .[52]

Truly, when I "see" someone in heaven, as I saw my ex-husband that day on the Mount of Beatitudes, I'm not losing my mind but righting the depth and breadth of my vision. When we strive to live the beatitudes here and now, a little bit of heaven is unleashed here and now.

There is a great spiritual umbilical cord pumping blood into the womb of this world. It is blood that was shed on the cross, blood that is poured out at every Mass, blood that is glorified in heaven. Truly, through the sacrifice of Christ on the cross, heaven is as intimately connected to us as the mother is to the child in her womb. Just so, God is invested in our flourishing, willing to go to any length to protect us——that is, to love and protect *you*.

The Most Sacred Space on Earth

I worked for nearly fourteen years at the Center for Catholic Studies on the University of St. Thomas campus in St. Paul, Minnesota. It was one of the greatest joys of my life—not only because the mission of the center was so close to my heart; not only because my colleagues, students, and friends there were stellar, brilliant, and delightful; but because of the Eucharist.

Two floors below my desk at the center, the Blessed Sacrament was in repose in our chapel. The altar was basically under my desk, and what a metaphor: to place my work on the altar each day. I felt that Jesus was literally supporting me all day long. Daily Mass was celebrated there, and the center, led by the students, hosted Eucharistic Adoration there every Monday.

How highly favored I felt to walk downstairs to go to Mass or to Adoration or to pray and to see so many students and colleagues there, on their knees, seeking the face of the Lord! It's a remarkable joy to go to Mass with one's colleagues, and there's nothing quite so heartening as seeing a young person, their whole beautiful life ahead of them, in Adoration. That purity keeps the world on its axis, no doubt.

I was keenly aware of what a privilege it was to work so close to the Blessed Sacrament, and I was loath to give that up. Alas, the time came when I had so many weekend retreats and speaking events that it was no longer feasible to show up on Monday at my desk. I needed to hand my position on to the next person. Oh, but I mourned that office, that regular proximity to Jesus in the Eucharist.

But the Lord provided. I kept a weekly holy hour at my parish, St. Pius X. One day, about a year before I left my job, the lovely woman who organized the schedule at St. Pius told me they were hoping to refresh the Adoration chapel. There were stains on the ceiling from a roof leak, the chairs and kneelers were faded, the rug was worn down to nothing. In short, the chapel needed a makeover. "I just want to create something beautiful for Jesus," the woman told me, and I knew exactly how she felt. I said, "I know just the man for that."

Several years earlier, I had married a very creative, faithful man. He is a gift from a merciful God, no doubt, and we are extremely well suited to one another. Life with him has been sweet, simple, and delightful. He happens to be an architect and has a particularly strong gift for reimagining spaces. A devout Catholic, he'd made a personal study of canon law in relation to sacred architecture and spaces and had spent numerous hours in that chapel already. He was the perfect man for a redesign.

He went to work with the chapel committee, bringing a new beauty, order, and simplicity to this sacred space. I was so excited; I would occasionally lean over his shoulder as he worked and remind him, "Just think; you're creating the most sacred space on earth! Think about what will happen there." I could barely wait to see what he would create for the Lord we both loved so much.

Not long ago, our archbishop came to bless this new Adoration chapel. Although I had to give up my proximity to the Blessed Sacrament when I left my job, I can now spend time with my Beloved in a space imagined by my other beloved, in a chapel less than a mile from my home. The Lord spoils me.

The world-renowned ALBL Oberammergau—wood-carvers from the Bavarian Alps, in business since 1556—created the statuary for the chapel, including the corpus on the crucifix. As I was praying there one day, admiring the carvings, looking especially at the face of Jesus, I noticed something unmistakable: Jesus on the cross is smiling.

What an extraordinary choice on behalf of the sculptor, I thought. How bold! I got on their website to see some of the other carvings, wondering if this was a common choice. It was not.

I have spent a considerable number of hours before this crucifix. Kneeling, seated, standing, bowing, and from every angle, I am convinced, Jesus is smiling from that cross. It's not a broad, gregarious grin, of course. It is much more subtle and serene, gentle and meek. I can imagine that he has just spoken this word, "It is finished." I can imagine him taking one last, lingering look at his mother, Mary, at Mary Magdalene, and at his dear friend John.

I can imagine that he, in perfect communion with his Father, is tasting the first drops of victory over sin and death. I can imagine joy in the midst of affliction, heaven peeking through to earth.

Monsignor Benson reminds us,

The one and only thing in human life that God desires to end is Sin. There is not a pure joy or a sweet human relationship or a selfless ambition or a divine hope which He does not desire to continue and to be crowned and transfigured beyond all ambition and all hope. On the contrary, He desires only to end that one single thing which ruins relationship and spoils joy and poisons aspirations.[53]

It is finished, indeed. Sin is conquered, indeed. Oh, but the love lives on forever—glorified, magnified. I think that is what must have put that tender smile on the crucified Christ.

Fr. Vann said, "To live in the present is to live in the Presence; to see Him in all things and to see all things, all situations, all moments, all interests and desires, in Him."[54] When next you pray before the cross, allow Jesus, the suffering servant, the innocent Lamb, to make his presence known to you.

But don't stop there. Invite Jesus—who is resurrected, glorified, all-powerful, all-merciful—to be present to you, too. Will you allow him to smile at you, even from the cross? Will you allow him to bring heaven's joy into the midst of your affliction?

It is finished, and because it is, you have what you need to lead a holy life. Because Jesus has accomplished all on the cross, mercy is available to you at every moment that you need it. Because of the sacrifice on Golgotha, you can build a meaningful life no matter what you suffer. You can taste heaven here and now, even in and through that suffering.

Look to Jesus on the cross; look to him in this word. Ask him to send you new blood of belief, new blood pulsing with robust, rich, living beatitude. Blood enough to convince you that, when you lose your life for Christ, you gain it, and abundantly so.

PROMPT FOR PRAYER

Made for Happiness

Did you know you were created for happiness, that happiness should be the prevailing sentiment of our lives as Christians? Fr. Vann reminds us:

> We should not be shy of the word "happy." We have been given the gospel of life. . . . To be suspicious of happiness and regard it as faintly irreligious is an unchristian thing—if you want to be a canonized saint, you must first become a notoriously happy person. . . . The beatitudes tell us how to be happy. . . . Happiness is not something to be searched for; still less is it something you can make; it is something you can only receive, and become.[55]

How happy are you? Do you need a beatific infusion?

I invite you to slowly reread the beatitudes. Pay attention interiorly as you read them. Which one attracts you the most? Rest in that beatitude for a moment. Then ask the Lord to give you a "beatific" glimpse of your life in which this beatitude is operating. What graces are being unleashed? How is the Lord blessing you? How is this a taste of heaven?

In the weeks ahead, work your way through all the beatitudes, praying with them one at a time and speaking to the Lord about how to make their graces more abundant in your daily life. Don't neglect repetition. Praying with one single beatitude on multiple occasions is an effective method of receiving its graces even more fully.

† † †

QUESTIONS FOR DISCUSSION OR JOURNALING

1. Is there a paradox of the faith that you struggle with? What is it, and what is the source of the tension you have around it?

2. Can you think of a time when you saw a beatitude in action? What happened, and what did it teach you?

3. Which of the beatitudes is your favorite, and why? Which of the beatitudes is hardest for you to imagine, and why?

4. Can you imagine your worst enemy in heaven with you? How would you be different? How would they be different?

CHAPTER 7

The Seventh and Final Word

"Father, into your hands I commit my spirit."
—*Luke 23:46, RSVCE*

One day during my prayer time, I decided to focus on this passage from the Gospel of John: "Whoever receives me receives the one who sent me" (John 13:20, NABRE). My meditation unfolded this way: [56]

I was with Jesus, and he wanted to take me to the Father, but I was afraid to go. I was afraid I'd be a disappointment or that, when the Father saw me, he'd be angry with me. I was afraid of his anger. I balked.

But Jesus took me by the hand and smiled at me. There was not an ounce of fear in his eyes, so I consented to be led. We entered a cave and descended into a very dark tunnel.

We were in a place that reminded me to the catacombs. I could barely see, but Jesus knew the way perfectly. He never let go of my hand, and his steps were sure, confident.

Finally the tunnel opened into a small room lit by torches around the perimeter. The Father was sitting there on a large, solid throne—very simple, almost plain, made of stone. His head was down, as if he were studying something on the floor.

Slowly he raised his head to look at me. I immediately darted behind Jesus, frightened.

But Jesus nudged me to look at the Father again. When I did, my breath caught: I saw Jesus, Jesus in the Father. Such a remarkable family resemblance!

A sense of wholeness I cannot describe filled the room, flowing between the Father and the Son. It was a weight and majesty that would overwhelm me completely but for Jesus, who still held my hand. The Father's eyes were dark and penetrating; they frightened me at first. As I looked more closely, I saw a million universes in them. All truth, all perfection, all holiness—I've never seen anything so terrifying, so beautiful, so alive all at once.

My words to Jesus were a whisper: "That's the *Father!*" I said. Though still afraid, still tucked behind Jesus, I saw the Father and Jesus exchange a knowing smile. I realized that I wanted to come back here—slowly and carefully and always with Jesus leading the way—but again and again, to the throne of the Father, *my Father*. In fact, there is nowhere else I would rather be. With Jesus holding my hand.

The Father Wound

Most of us carry some version of a "father wound." But Jesus makes it plain: he is the way to the Father, and he's also the way to healing any father wound we might carry.

Do you struggle to believe in the Father's care for you, to believe that he delights in you and wishes to bless you? Can you allow Jesus, in this last word, to take you by the hand

and make an introduction? To show you the Father he knows, serves, loves, and trusts with his very life?

The first last word of Christ takes us directly to the Father: "Father, forgive them, they know not what they do" (Luke 23:34, NABRE). How appropriate that the final word should return our attention to the Father, inviting us to glimpse the radical intimacy between Father and Son and to wonder about the implications of this union for our own lives! In essence, to ask, How closely am I knitted to the Father? Do I trust him?

"Father, into your hands I commit my spirit," Jesus says, but in truth, his spirit has never been anywhere else. His will has never been anything other than the Father's will. The Father and Son live in perfect harmony. How often does Jesus remind us of their connection, that in fact he has come to show us the Father?

John's Gospel is especially sensitive to this. Jesus says, "Whoever has seen me has seen the Father" (14:9); "I am not alone because the Father is with me" (16:32); and "The Son can do nothing on his own, but only what he sees the Father doing; for whatever the Father does, the Son does likewise" (5:19).

In turn, the Father lays claim to his Son. He breaks through the veil of heaven to announce, at Jesus' baptism, "This is my Son, the Beloved, with whom I am well pleased" (Matthew 3:17). And later, at the transfiguration, the Father tells the three disciples present, "Listen to him" (17:5). The loving consonance between Father and Son cannot be ignored, overemphasized, or refuted.

"Jesus lives in the presence of the Father," wrote Romano Guardini. "This proximity is brought about by the Father's will and Jesus' obedience. There is a unison of love in this nearness; and in this unison, there is a joy and the most ineffable peace." He added, "The presence of His Father is so close to our Lord, and His oneness with Him such an interior thing, that the living Jesus Christ is simply the Father become visible."[57]

Jesus' final word from the cross is not simply an invitation to grow in obedience to the voice of the Father, to surrender ourselves to his will. Above all else, it is an invitation to enter into and to receive a share in the sacred unity of the Father through the Son—where we find peace, joy, and blessing. It is an invitation to discover the Father by watching the Son. In essence, it is an invitation for us, children of God, to come home.

Hope for the Prodigal

How can we enter into such unity with the Father if we do not trust him—if we fear him, are indifferent to him, disrespect him, mock him as inessential or absurd, or even hate him? How can we ever return to the house of our Father if we are not reconciled to him?

"We must," wrote Pope Benedict, "let Jesus teach us what *father* really means."[58]

I read not long ago that scientists have made some advances in their efforts to fertilize a woman's egg without sperm, using only matter from the bodies of women. The implication, or so the article quipped, is that men could become obsolete. Leaving the medical ethics of such an experiment aside, I wonder how is it that fatherhood—and men in general—came to be under attack, reduced to nothingness? What could be more devastating than to be proclaimed obsolete?

We've become one big prodigal culture that says, "Father, you are obsolete to me. Your money, I'll take, but you I will leave behind as nonessential." This was an illusion that the prodigal son of the Gospel of Luke could not sustain, nor can we (see 15:11-32).

As often as we hear that our culture has failed women—and certainly it has—we cannot ignore the damage it has inflicted on men. Examples are everywhere but perhaps nowhere more evident than in our federal prison system. In the year 2017, according to the Federal Bureau of Prisons, 93.2 percent of those in US prisons were men. Women are far less likely than men to be incarcerated if convicted of a serious crime, nearly 50 percent less likely. Some studies suggest that these figures are not evidence that men are more criminal by design but that there is an institutional bias against them.[59]

Surely these data must tell us something about the ways we are failing our nation's sons and helping perpetuate a blight of fatherlessness in our culture. According to a recent US census, 17.4 million children live in fatherless homes, many of them in poverty.[60] Studies suggest that young men raised in father-less households have a far greater chance of being involved in criminal activity.

Given this landscape, can it be any more obvious that men and fatherhood are under siege? Indeed, Satan hates the human person. How clever a tactic it is to attack fathers and watch the rest of the family crumble in despair.

Even in the case of strong fathers, no man is perfect. It seems no one escapes, at least in some way, a father wound: some way in which the one who was entrusted with their care, the one of whom they had a legal, natural, and spiritual right to that care, failed.

Through absence, indifference, betrayal, neglect, shaming, criticizing, or perhaps full-out abuse, some of us have learned to fear, hate, or mistrust our fathers. To a greater or lesser degree, these wounds need healing. It seems there is a connection between the father wounds we carry and the corresponding assault on men—treating fatherhood as an irredeemable category, a failed state. And whether we mean to or not, sometimes we cast this whole messy assessment onto our heavenly Father.

We must work to retrieve our understanding of fatherhood as it is revealed to us through the Father and the Son. Fatherhood language is not something we conjured up or projected onto God; God as Father is revealed and given in the Old Testament and made even clearer in the New Testament. This is not an arbitrary issue. Jesus teaches us to pray to "Abba, Father!" (Romans 8:15, NABRE), and as we have established, he consistently claims his identity as Son of the Father. And this is a Father he *trusts*: "Into your hands—in this most vulnerable moment of my life, my death—I entrust myself to you, Father."

We want our heavenly Father to teach us what real fatherhood is—through his Son. Furthermore, we want to allow the Lord to bind up not only our own father wounds but all the wounds our culture has inflicted on fatherhood. In some ways, this is the great work of Jesus: he came to "re-father" the world. He came to introduce us to a supreme Father, a Father who has his heart set on every one of us.

Love Letters from the Father[61]

When I was quite young, I lost a job due to layoffs. It jolted me to suddenly be out of work, and I asked my father to help me navigate this difficult situation. I was, no doubt, a bit of a drama queen, and I felt like a hapless victim of the cold, cruel universe. I knew I needed to address that thinking immediately, or I'd soon become "attitudinally challenged."

My father, a judge, had recently retired from the bench. For fifty years he got up every day and put on a suit and tie and went to work. He spent his whole career in law, helping carry the pain of lost souls, broken families, and abandoned children. My father took his work seriously, and I always thought of him as somewhat tough. I knew he wouldn't let me get away with the "poor me" bit for too long, and so I turned to him for encouragement and guidance.

I called my father and proposed the following assignment: "Buy a pile of postcards, address them all to me, and send one every day for several weeks. Write on the first line: 'You are not a victim' and, on the second, 'You are (blank),' filling in the blank with some positive attribute you see in me, some talent or gift God has given me." My father accepted this mission enthusiastically.

Just a few days later, I went to the post office to check my mailbox. When I opened it up and saw a postcard waiting

"

We want to allow the Lord to bind up not only our own father wounds but all the wounds our culture has inflicted on father-hood. In some ways, this is the great work of Jesus: he came to "re-father" the world.

there with my father's handwriting, I began weeping (much to the dismay of the other postal customers, I might add). It wasn't just his willingness to support me that touched me, nor was it the fact that he didn't think I was a no-talent victim in a hapless, hopeless universe. It proved to me in a moving and personal way that "not one [sparrow] falls to the ground without your Father's knowledge" (Matthew 10:29, NABRE).

Jesus constantly reminds us that no one knows us better than the Father. He created us, he is intimately acquainted with our needs, and he is more than dedicated to meeting every one of them—whether it be food for the table, fulfilling work, the relief of a cool breeze on a hot summer day, or something as simple and free as a word of encouragement from a concerned father to his distressed daughter.

The real surprise in this little experiment came from my father. He completely embraced the project, embellishing it with far more zeal, humor, and creativity than I expected. One of his more memorable openers was, "Victim . . . NOT!" Many of the gifts and talents he listed, I never even knew he noticed or thought about.

At one point Dad wrote, "I always thought all of these things: I guess I just never said them." In the rigors of providing for seven children, he wasn't always able to stop and tell us directly how much he cared about us. But through our *discours de cartes postales*, he reminded me that—like Jesus, like my heavenly Father—he was acutely interested in everything going on in my life at any time.

How much more is that true of my heavenly Father.

At another point in my life, I was struggling mightily to decide between law school and a master's degree in fine arts in writing.[62] I called my father and lamented, swinging fitfully between the two options. Law seemed so practical and useful; writing seemed a bit romantic and not the least bit practical. What should I do? Dad's response changed the course of my life.

He said, "I think you would make a very good lawyer. You love to reason, to build arguments, and you would be very good at that." I thought he might be finished, but then he continued, "But when you *write*," and he paused a moment, searching for the right words, "I don't even know where that *comes* from." His voice carried something in it like reverence, something like amazement, a touch of paternal pride. "It seems to me," he went on, "that *that* is something very special."

I'll never forget that moment. I was flooded not just with permission but with a reverent kind of encouragement to be exactly who I was created to be. In that moment I recognized that writing was a calling, not a dalliance. It needed to be taken seriously, to be cultivated and nourished. It had import and purpose.

Furthermore, my father's confidence that I had received something special, despite the fact that this specialness set me apart from him—that I would pursue a path very different from his—was more freeing than I can express. He trusted in God's plans for my flourishing, and he understood that meant something far more important than making money, becoming famous, or taking the safest road.

The words of Jeremiah, that fiery prophet, sing in my soul. I believe in them deeply—for me and for you—because this is the Father I am coming to know.

> For surely I know the plans I have for you, says the LORD, plans for your welfare and not for harm, to give you a future with hope. Then when you call upon me and come and pray to me, I will hear you. When you search for me, you will find me; if you seek me with all your heart, *I will let you find me*, says the LORD. (Jeremiah 29:11-14, emphasis mine)

This is indeed the Father that Jesus Christ on the cross knew. This is indeed the Father he allowed to name him, guide him, bring about the greatest possible good from his life, and then bring him home.

When we allow the Father to find us—when we allow him to help us find our true selves, to discover what we've been created for—we flourish. We come home to ourselves.

On the cross, Jesus trusted his Father with good reason. The Father knows our needs—intimately, personally, profoundly. He does not let our suffering fall fallow. If our needs are not being met in a situation, it doesn't mean the Father doesn't care. As we've noted, our pain, rightly understood, can bring some greater good to the world and to us. In the case of my own father and his loving postcards, the greater good was a renewed relationship with him and a renewed relationship with myself. I came to understand myself and my gifts in a completely new way, in a way that empowered me.

Even more importantly, the Father names us and claims us. It seems to me that this action fits within the very essence of fatherhood: naming his creation. In Scripture this is one of the great goods that men bring into the world, starting with Adam, who walks through the garden taking stock of every creature—what they do, what they are for—and naming them carefully. In fact, he names Eve, too (see Genesis 2:20; 3:20). Jesus names Peter his rock, the rock on which he will build his Church (see Matthew 16:18).

It is the Father's joy to claim us as sons and daughters and then to give us work in his kingdom. If our earthly fathers have fallen down in providing for us, in helping us find our way in the world, we can turn, just as Jesus did at every moment of his life, to our heavenly Father. We can ask him to father us. He will do so with joy and passion.

Let me speak plainly to fathers for a moment: you will never be obsolete. Your children will always need you to speak your blessing and affirmation over them, to help give life to their hopes and dreams. In this way you bear the image and likeness of God the Father. What could be more necessary, more sacred?

Coming Home

In the past years, I have traveled from Portland, Oregon, to Portland, Maine, and many places in between, giving talks and retreats. It's a tremendous privilege to travel, to meet faithful men and women who are seeking the face of the Lord, and to encounter the unique colors and rhythms of different parishes and regions. I love what I do, even the hard parts—like airports and packing and hotel rooms.

But one of my favorite parts of traveling for ministry is coming home. When my husband can pick me up at the airport, my homecoming starts there. As he rounds the corner to the baggage claim area to collect me, I feel already the relief and rest of coming home. Just getting into the car with him, my blood pressure drops, and my body relaxes. He is home for me, vocationally speaking, so where he is, I am home in a very real sense.

When my husband and I were hunting for our first home together, the market was brutal. Even ramshackle houses sold almost instantly, with owners often calling for highest and best offers the first day the house was on the market. Many buyers were paying as much as 30 percent over the asking price. My husband and I weren't interested in overpaying. It wouldn't be prudent or just, and my husband has a truly refined sense of justice. It's one of my favorite things about him.

I found a somewhat geriatric house in a good neighborhood. The whole house tilted a bit—less dramatically than the Tower of Pisa, but still. The porch was rotten in places, and the rooms were small. The house had a root cellar instead of a basement, and in order to get to it, we would have to climb down a rickety ladder. This might have been a touch romantic when I was younger, but at this point, the idea of descending into a root cellar on an uncertain ladder was not a winning idea.

Still, the property was a corner lot on a quiet street in a neighborhood we knew. It had a very large garage with extra work benches, which I knew would appeal to my husband. Mature trees provided great shade and beauty. I told the Lord I'd be grateful for this little house if it was his will, and I made an appointment to see it. By the time of the showing, the owners were already receiving offers far above their asking price.

This pattern of house hunting went on for a while. We looked at houses in our price range that had serious flaws, only to find they'd sold for too much and far too quickly than my extremely thoughtful husband would find acceptable. I spent more than a few hours walking through homes, telling the Lord, "We could make this work if we had to."

There was the house with a serious foundation issue that my husband spotted instantly. Another had a strange smell—making us wonder where the body was buried! Another, though charming, was extremely small and situated far too close to a busy four-lane street. The living room rumbled and buzzed with the traffic whizzing past. Even with these serious drawbacks, these homes disappeared from the market with incredible speed.

"Every home is a compromise," I told myself and the Lord. "We can make something work."

Then one day I spotted a sweet little house on a dead-end street. It called to me. I made an appointment to see it. It was modest and fairly priced, and the previous owners had refurbished it in ways that were acceptable and helpful. And it was close enough to my husband's work that he could come home for lunch every day.

This house had more than enough space, gleaming original wood floors, and two fireplaces. There was a huge new deck with a view of the lake behind it. The rooms were bright and had wonderful light. One room I pegged almost instantly as my writing and prayer room, something I had been dreaming of my entire life. I loved this little house and could see ourselves in it. I tried not to get my hopes up, and in fact it had been sold before we even set foot inside.

Over the next week, I sulked. (My poor husband.) "We'll never find a house!" I pouted. It was Holy Thursday of the year of COVID. That evening we watched Mass online-how dreadful. This denial of "real Mass" on such a holy day only compounded my self-pity. I went to bed early in a terrible brood.

The next morning, Good Friday, my husband and I had a long and, on his part, very patient and forgiving conversation. I adjusted my attitude. Then something interesting happened: the house came back on the market. The first offer had fallen through.

We toured the house once more on Good Friday, made a reasonable offer that evening, and had it accepted on Holy Saturday. I will always think of this house as the Father's Easter present to us. On the feast of the Sacred Heart, we had it blessed and consecrated to the Sacred Heart.

Life here has been extremely sweet and satisfying. I've never before felt so safe and content. I am so at home. The other day I rode my bike past the leaning Tower of Pisa house and thought to myself, "I would have settled for so much less than what the Father had in mind. So much less."

This is the Father we must recover: the Father who, like the prodigal son's father, wants to give the very best gifts to his children: the fatted calf, the best robe, the ring for his finger. The devil wants to keep us wallowing in the pigsty, but the Father has plans for our flourishing and for our homecoming. He plans a feast for us.

In effect, this is what Jesus is doing in this final word: he is coming home. He can do that so supremely because he has never left the presence of his Father. Fr. Stinissen makes an excellent point:

> We cannot put our lives into God's hands demanding that his will be done in just one choice. That is wrong. Often we do not get a clear answer when we ask God questions in prayer. We can stand there just as perplexed after prayer as before. The secret of evangelical freedom from care is not that we surrender our life to God only at certain times. The secret is rather that we never leave God! Let your whole life rest in his powerful yet tender hand.[63]

Just as Jesus did, even on the cross.

When I am tempted toward self-centeredness, I can adapt Jesus' word to my prayer: "Into your hand, Father, I recommit my spirit." It's another way of saying, "I belong to you, I always have, and I always will." When I am tempted to make my vocation all about me and not about him: "Into your hands, Father, I commit my spirit." When I fear he has left me to my own devices: "Into your hands, Father . . ." When I am tempted to imagine that the Father is not present in my suffering: "Into your hands, Father . . ." When I need to remember who I am in Christ, "Into your hands, Father, I commit my life, my spirit, my heart, my hope, and my future."

PROMPT FOR PRAYER

Healing the Father Wound: Retrieving Holy Fatherhood

Many years ago, as I was coming back into the Church, I struggled to pray the traditional Rosary. I was not very skilled at prayer, and I'm sure that was part of the problem. But the mysteries were just falling flat on my heart. I didn't know how to engage them.

Then one day someone gave me a wonderful coffee-table book, *Mary, Images of the Virgin in Art* (BCL Press, 1998). It's a collection of some of the most beloved and well-known images of Mary ever painted, sketched, or sculpted. Many of the works capture the various mysteries of the Rosary. And so when I wanted to pray the Rosary, I would open this lovely book, find an image that centered on the appropriate mystery, and begin my decade with that sacred art, allowing it to focus my imagination and stir my heart. It was then that the Rosary began to open up for me, like a beautiful flower. Indeed, sacred art has long been an effective way to enter into contemplation of divine truths.

I have been inviting you throughout these pages to use your imagination as you pray with Scripture. If you find that difficult or dry, adding a sacred image to your prayer exercise might be a useful tool. As an example, find an image of Jesus blessing the children, one that appeals to you. Spend a few moments resting with that image. Take in the colors, the light and dark.

Take note of who is present. How are they responding to the presence of Jesus? What is Jesus doing?

Then slowly read the following passage:

> And they were bringing children to him, that he might touch them; and the disciples rebuked them. But when Jesus saw it he was indignant, and said to them, "Let the children come to me, do not hinder them; for to such belongs the kingdom of God. Truly, I say to you, whoever does not receive the kingdom of God like a child shall not enter it." And he took them in his arms and blessed them, laying his hands upon them. (Mark 10:13-16, RSVCE)

Imagine that your parents have brought you to Jesus for a blessing. Imagine them sending you forward to receive his blessing. How does he react when he sees you? How does he receive you? What happens for you interiorly when you see Jesus calling you forward? When he lays his hand of blessing on you, what do you sense he is saying to you? How do you respond?

There are, of course, innumerable ways in which the Father makes himself present to us. I have selected just a few ideas that might help you begin your prayer. If your prayer falls flat, try finding an image that portrays the Scripture verse you've chosen for meditation, and begin your prayer with that.

When you need a Father who will gently bless you:
 † Mark 10:13-16: Jesus blesses the children.

When you need a Father who will teach and guide you:
  † Mark 9:33-37: Jesus defines true greatness.

When you need a Father who believes in you:
  † Matthew 5:14-16: You are the light of the world.

When you need a Father who heals:
  † Mark 5:21-43: Jesus heals a woman and Jairus's daughter.

When you need a Father who will rescue and protect you:
  † Luke 15:1-7: Jesus tells the parable of the lost sheep.

When you need a Father who will nourish and prune you:
  † John 15:1-11: My Father is the vinedresser.

When you need a Father who forgives:
  † John 8:3-11: a sinful woman is forgiven.
  † Luke 15:11-32: Jesus tells the parable of the prodigal son.

When you need a Father who will bring you back to life:
  † John 11:1-44: Jesus brings Lazarus back to life.

† † †

QUESTIONS FOR DISCUSSION OR JOURNALING

1. Is there an area in your life that you would like to entrust to the Father's care, through Jesus? What is it? What obstacles keep you from entrusting this to him?

2. Can you think of a time when you had a distinct sense of the Father's presence in your life? What happened, and how did it affect you?

3. Do you feel at home with the Father? Why or why not?

4. What attributes does Jesus "make visible" in the Father? What attributes strike you the most, and why?

Epilogue

On the day I finish this book, it is early September and unusually warm for Minnesota. The sun is yawning one long last time over us before she retreats for winter. I hop on my bike and ride to a favorite spot on the edge of a large lake, where I can listen to the surf, feel the breeze, and pray.

Sailboats are anchored near the shore. A young family sits on the end of a dock, dangling legs and feet and toes in the water. The ducks are diving, thrusting their little duck rumps into the air—in a way that is rather amusing—while they look for fish snacks below. A few leaves on the trees around the lake are just beginning to yellow.

And I know, soon enough, the sun will withdraw her warmth just enough for this glistening lake to freeze over. And before I know it, I'll be walking across it with my puppies, where they will race and roll and sniff to their hearts' content until the bitter chill drives us back indoors.

So it is with the Lord. The work of the crucifixion is complete, and now he shall descend into darkness, withdraw himself from us just long enough to do what only he can do there. We can trust what the Lord does in his descent. When darkness falls on me, I know and trust that Jesus is still at work, doing what only he can do in me, even if I cannot perceive it.

We began these meditations by acknowledging that new life often begins in total darkness. With the final word of Christ on the cross, we find ourselves entering a new period of desolation indeed, one we commemorate each Holy Thursday evening by removing the Blessed Sacrament from the tabernacle and leaving the door open. Thus we can contemplate the emptiness.

In those days of entombment, Jesus may feel lost to us. But we mustn't imagine that this hidden mystery is some kind of inertia. Let us rest in the fact that even in his descent, Jesus accomplishes the Father's will. And the Father's will always results in truth, beauty, and goodness.

Let's not shrink from feelings of having lost our Lord either. It was this sense, this tremendous mourning of love lost, that drove Magdalene to search for Jesus at the tomb, and we know what happened there. Though she was looking for him, it was Jesus who found her.

In moments when we are looking for Jesus, in moments when he may feel lost to us, let's turn our hearts toward the light of Easter morning. Let's trust that soon—so soon—the Lord of all creation will appear in glory and call us by name. Nothing—not death, not sin, not all the powers of hell unleashed—will keep him from those he calls his own.

Notes

1. A version of this meditation appeared in Blessed Is She's Lenten supplement, *Here, Too: Where We Meet God*, Lent 2020.

2. See Robert Hugh Benson, *Paradoxes of Catholicism* (Monee, IL: Shepherd Publications, 2015), 135.

3. Roch O. Kereszty, OCist, *Jesus Christ: Fundamentals of Christology,* 3rd ed. (Staten Island, NY: Society of St. Paul's, 2002,) 24.

4. A version of this story was published in my article, "A Choice to Live: When the Unthinkable Happens, One Woman Learns 'Evil Can't Take Everything,'" *The Catholic Spirit*, September 14, 2020.

5. See Pope Benedict XVI, *Jesus of Nazareth, Holy Week: From the Entrance into Jerusalem to the Resurrection* (San Francisco, CA: Ignatius Press, 2011), 211.

6. Pope Benedict XVI, *Jesus of Nazareth, Holy Week*, 84, emphasis mine.

7. See St. Augustine, *Confessions*, book 8.29.

8. Augustin-Michel Lemonnier, *Light over the Scaffold: Prison Letters of Jacques Fesch* and *Cell 18: Unedited Letters of Jacques Fesch*, trans. Sr. Mary Thomas Noble (Staten Island, NY: Society of St. Paul, 1996), 9.

9. Lemonnier, *Scaffold*, 19.

10. Lemonnier, *Scaffold*, 20.

11. Lemonnier, *Cell 18*, 235.

12. Lemonnier, *Cell*, 246.

13. Lemonnier, *Scaffold*, 27.

14. Lemonnier, *Scaffold*, 27.

15. Lemonnier, *Scaffold*, 29–30.

16. Lemonnier, *Scaffold*, 98.

17. Lemonnier, *Scaffold*, 87.

18. Lemonnier, *Cell*, 244–45.

19. Lemonnier, *Scaffold*, 73.

20. Lemonnier, *Scaffold, 109*.

21. Timothy M. Gallagher, OMV, *Meditation and Contemplation: An Ignatian Guide to Praying with Scripture* (New York: Crossroads Publishing, 2008), 36.

22. Fr. Richard Veras, *Jesus of Israel: Finding Christ in the Old Testament* (Cincinnati, OH: Servant, 2007), 131.

23. Gerald Vann, OP, *The Divine Pity: A Study in the Social Implications of the Beatitudes* (New York: Sheed & Ward, 1946), 144.

24. Ignatius of Loyola, *The Spiritual Exercises and Selected Works* (Mahwah, New Jersey: Paulist Press, 1991), 197.

25. Pope Benedict XVI, *Jesus of Nazareth* (New York: Crown Publishing Group, 2007), 221.

26. Edith Stein, *Essays on Woman*, (ICS Publications, 2012), 8.

27. Pope John Paul II, *Mulieris Dignitatem* [On the Dignity and Vocation of Women], August 15, 1988, 30, http://www.vatican.va/content/john-paul-ii/en/apost_letters/1988/documents/hf_jp-ii_apl_19880815_mulieris-dignitatem.html"www.vatican.va/content/john-paul-ii/en/apost_letters/1988/documents/hf_jp-ii_apl_19880815_mulieris-dignitatem.html, emphasis in original.

28. John Paul II, 30.

29. Joseph Ratzinger, *Daughter Zion: Meditations on the Church's Marian Belief* (San Francisco: Ignatius, 1983), 17.

30. Gallagher, 36.

31. Joseph Pronechen, "50 Wise and Wonderful Insights from Padre Pio," *National Catholic Register*, September 23, 2019, https://www.ncregister.com/blog/50-wise-and-wonderful-insights-from-padre-pio.

32. To see St. John's drawing of the crucifix, go to aleteia.org/2017/09/22/discover-the-crucifix-drawn-by-saint-john-of-the-cross-after-a-mystical-vision/.

33. Wilfrid Stinissen, *Nourished by the Word: Reading the Bible Contemplatively*, trans. Joseph b. Board, JD, PhD (Ligouri, MO: Ligouri Publications, 1999), 77.

34. See Fr. Paul Murray, *I Loved Jesus in the Night: Teresa of Calcutta—A Secret Revealed* (Brewster, MA: Paraclete, 2020), 47–49. I included a slightly different version of this story in my book *Jesus Approaches: What Contemporary Women Can Learn about Healing, Freedom & Joy from the Women of the New Testament* (Chicago: Loyola Press, 2017), 88.

35. *Mother Teresa: Come Be my Light: The Private Writings of the Saint of Calcutta*, ed. Brian Kolodiejchuk, MC (New York: Image Books, 2009), 38.

36. Benson, 50.

37. Wilfrid Stinissen, *Into Your Hands, Father: Abandoning Ourselves to the God Who Loves Us*, trans. Sr. Clare Marie, OCD (San Francisco: Ignatius Press, 2011), 41.

38. Vann, 149.

39. Vann, 153.

40. George Weigel, *The End and the Beginning: Pope John Paul II—The Victory of Freedom, the Last Years, the Legacy* (New York: Doubleday, 2010) 371,

41. See Pope John Paul II, *Salvifici Doloris* [On the Christian Meaning of Human Suffering], February 11, 1984, 29, www.vatican.va/content/john-paul-ii/en/apost_letters/1984/documents/hf_jp-ii_apl_11021984_salvifici-doloris.html.

42. Fr. Paul Murray, *I Loved Jesus in the Night: Theresa of Calcutta-A Secret Revealed* (Brewster, MA: Paraclete Press, 2016), 68.

43. Stinissen, *Nourished by the Word*, 86.

44. Thomas Merton, *Praying the Psalms* (Collegeville, MN: The Liturgical Press, 1956), 8.

45. Stinissen, *Nourished by the Word*, 86.

46. Kereszty, 383, emphasis mine.

47. Kereszty, 383.

48. Margaret Ferris, CSJ, *Compassioning: Basic Counseling Skills for Christian Caregivers* (Eugene, OR: Wipf and Stock Publishers, 2010), v, emphasis mine.

49. Pope Benedict XVI, *Jesus of Nazareth: From the Baptism in the Jordan to the Transfiguration*, trans. Adrian J. Walker (New York: Doubleday, 2007), 26.

50. Vann, 150.

51. Benedict VI, *Jesus of Nazareth*, 72.

52. Peter Kreeft, *Heaven: The Heart's Deepest Longing* (San Francisco, CA: Ignatius Press, 1980), 172, 174.

53. Benson, 67.

54. Vann, 24.

55. Vann, 16–17.

56. A version of this meditation was published as "Receive the Father," May 12, 2022, Blessed Is She Devotions, https://blessedisshe.net/devotions/receive-the-father/.

57. Romano Guardini, *The Inner Life of Jesus: Pattern of All Holiness* (Manchester, NH: Sophia Institute Press, 1992), 86.

58. Benedict XVI, *Jesus of Nazareth*, 136.

59. Dyfed Leosche, "The Prison Gender Gap," *Statista*, https://www.statista.com/chart/11573/gender-of-inmates-in-us-federal-prisons-and-general-population/ Accessed October 1, 2022.

60. Szabolcs Szecsei, "20 Statistics on Fatherless Homes and the Importance of Dads," *Modern Gentleman*, January 7, 2021, moderngentlemen.net/statistics-on-fatherless-homes/.

61. This section appeared in a slightly different form in my article "Love Letters from the Father," *Our Sunday Visitor*, June 20, 1999.

62. I have published several iterations of this story. First as "What Dads Do" in my monthly column, "Your Heart, His Home," *The Catholic Spirit*, June 2021, and later in Blessed Is She's book *Made New: 52 Devotions for Catholic Women* (Nashville, TN: HarperCollins, 2021), 187–88.

63. Stinissen, *Into Your Hands*, 55, quoting Martin Lönnebo.

About the Author

Liz Kelly is a popular speaker and an award-winning author of ten books, including *Love like a Saint, Reasons I Love Being Catholic*, which won the Catholic Press Association First Place award for Best Popular Presentation of the Faith in 2007, and *Jesus Approaches: What Contemporary Women Can Learn about Healing, Freedom and Joy from the Women of the New Testament*, which has won a number of awards, including Best Book in the Religion/Christianity category for 2017-2019. Her written works frequently appear in the Magnificat's Lenten and Advent Companions and in other Catholic venues, including Catholic Spirit, Blessed is She, and Jesuitprayer.org.

Her monthly column, Your Heart, His Home, is published throughout the US. Kelly has appeared on Relevant Radio, Catholic Answers, Radio Maria, Public Radio, Boston Catholic Television, EWTN, and Salt and Light Television. From 2008 to 2012, she was the managing editor of *Logos: A Journal of Catholic Thought and Culture*, published through the Center for Catholic Studies at the University of St. Thomas and cohost along with David Deavel of the podcast, Deep Down Things (deepdownthings/patreon.com). She and her husband, Vincent, an architect, live in Minnesota. Find out more at LizK.org.

JESUS
APPROACHES

||||||||||||||||||||||||||||||||||||||||||||||||||||||||||||||||||||||||||||

A Study for Women

—NOW AVAILABLE TO TAKE HOME—

Nine Sessions *of* Prayer, Study, *and* Inspiration

IN HER BOOK *Jesus Approaches*, award-winning Minnesota author Liz Kelly shares vivid stories of New Testament women whose encounters with Jesus freed them to flourish in life. The stories are supplemented with moving accounts from her own life, and from the lives of women like you, to demonstrate that sometimes the best way to find healing, strength, and wholeness in Christ is, ironically, to lead with vulnerability and openness.

The *Jesus Approaches* Take-Home Retreat guides individuals or groups through the book in nine contemplative sessions. Each session includes a forty-minute talk by Liz, which is accompanied by the quotes, insights, and discussion/journaling questions in the *Jesus Approaches Supplement*.

The Take-Home Retreat is designed to strengthen your relationship to Christ and the women who knew and loved him so well, while also refining your ability to pray with Scripture. Participants have called it "transformative," "intimate and completely engaging," and "a sensitive look at how Jesus interacts with women in Scripture and therefore, how He interacts with me."

LizK.org *flourish in your faith*

Praise for *Love like a Saint*

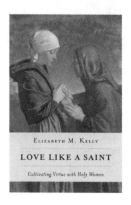

ELIZABETH M. KELLY

LOVE LIKE A SAINT

Cultivating Virtue with Holy Women

"This book is a source of encouragement and hope for those pursuing holiness in their own lives. I recommend it wholeheartedly."
—The Most Rev. Andrew H. Cozzens S.T.D., D.D., Auxiliary Bishop of the Archdiocese of St. Paul and Minneapolis

"*Love like a Saint* challenges today's women to see the story that Jesus is weaving in our own lives, and to respond to his grace with the small, daily acts of love that are the stepping stones to eternal joy."
—Colleen Carroll Campbell, author of *The Heart of Perfection*

"This book will lead you to a deepening love of virtue—not one of obligation, but a desire to look more and more like the Lord."
—Jenna Guizar, founder and creative director of Blessed Is She